Corporate Characters

Wulf Rehder

Corporate Characters

52 Shades of Business

www.tredition.de

Copyright © 2017   Wulf Rehder

Verlag: tredition GmbH, Hamburg, Germany

ISBN Paperback: 978-3-7439-6281-1
ISBN Hardcover: 978-3-7439-6282-8
ISBN e-Book: 978-3-7439-6283-5

Printed in Germany

For Carol
Kai and Toki

"This book should either be required reading in every American corporation, or it should be forbidden. It contains too much truth."

> Email message from a vice president of a US corporation, responding to the first edition of this book, in 1989

Content

Introduction:

II. Advanced Characters

The A-B-C of Corporate Characters

Some say that every man (and woman) belongs to one of two camps: the faculty of scientists or the fraternity of writers and artists. In the late 1800s, this dichotomy pitched Thomas Henry Huxley against Matthew Arnold, and in 1959, C.P. Snow coined the phrase of the "two cultures." He described the rift as a breakdown of communication between the humanist tradition and the scientific worldview. The critic F. R. Leavis didn't agree and called Snow's thesis a "public relations" stunt for the sciences. The wealthy Templeton Foundation, in its ambition to mediate, has spent much grant money, including a lavishly endowed Templeton Prize, for interdisciplinary studies pacifying the two factions under the umbrella of Spirituality, in an attempt to reconcile the profits from the sciences with the promises of religion. Predictably, this ambitious effort has led to a motley crew of Prize winners, including Mother Teresa, Freeman Dyson, Billy Graham and Alvin Plantinga. In the groves of European academe, the French philosopher Hadot has tried to overcome Snow's chasm by depicting the two traditions, which he calls the *Promethean* and the *Orphic*, as autonomous but interdependent styles of reasoning about the world, a dual endeavor allegedly underway since Heraclitus. Over the years, several prominent intellectuals have offered their thoughts about a "third culture" bridging the divide identified by Snow. Examples of such diplomatic efforts can be found in publications by The Edge Foundation (see edge.org). But alas! These efforts have only resulted in awkward compromises with titles like humanist sciences and scientific humanism.

11

The book in your hands is about a truly different third culture and its practitioners. I call them Corporate Characters. The intellectual noise and polemical dust created by the quibbling between scientific and literary men has obscured a simple fact: Just as every bar stool needs three legs in order to be stable, so have people since times immemorial relied on three pillars to stabilize their life: the above two, science and humanities, and a third one: business. While the modern-day protagonists for the sciences and humanities, professors, artists, writers, have been the subjects of much scholarship, the representative of business, the *homme d'affaires*, has so far been sorely neglected.

Uncovering this third basic style of thought and action is as important as Einstein's discovery of the warped universe as the third world system in addition to the "two Major Systems of the World" described by Galileo. Continuing this analogy, we might say that the Ptolemaic system corresponds to the traditional culture of the *homme des lettres*, while the Copernican revolution led to the enlightenment, which in turn hatched modern science. Several hundred years later, Einstein taught us his theory about curved space-time, which is the cosmological equivalent of the known fact that in business there are many crooked roads and detours based on the theory that time is money.

It is obvious that after the ages of Ptolemy and Copernicus, we now live squarely in the third culture, the age of business and economics. The businessman has truly arrived. From the sciences he carves his high-technology tools, from the arts he plucks his entertainment. The quest for eternal Truth and the search for heavenly Beauty has been replaced with the Law of Supply and Demand. Within this new framework, "what's true" has been demoted to "what's useful", and "what's beautiful" translates as "what's attractive." The new kind of ever-changing business "Truth" reflects the ups and downs of the stock market, and the new market-driven "Beauty" is as fickle as fashion.

Though it exploits the sciences and the arts, our current business culture can no longer simply be defined in terms of the two older "two Major Systems of the World." Business stands proudly by itself, and its practitioners must be portrayed and judged on their own merit.

Such a phenomenology of Corporate Characters has been attempted in the book you are about to read. It was inspired by Theophrastus' book *Characters*, written some twenty-three centuries ago, and by Elias Canetti's whimsical psychological types portrayed in *Earwitness: Fifty Characters* (1979, originally published in German in 1974). Two of Theophrastus' characters, the Loquacious and the Busybody, freely translated and suitably adapted, are included in this collection of Corporate Characters. Through personal experience, wide ranging interviews, and bookish (though very enjoyable) research, I have found that all those wild and wily, tame and timid, high and mighty inmates of a contemporary business bestiary can be described within a systematic framework that derives it unique language and defining concepts from just three sources: Americana, Biblica, and Classica, the A-B-C of business culture. By Americana, I mean, for instance, the folk tales of John Henry, the Constitution, and the economic philosophy of Henry David Thoreau. Under Biblica, I count references to biblical stories and their heroes such as Moses and his field managers. Finally, Classica allude to the root of American business in Shakespeare's plays and, farther back still, to the Athenian water cooler, where greenhorns listened to Socrates holding forth.

This portfolio of business archetypes contains 52 snapshots of corporate characters, one for each week in the fiscal year, or one for each card in a full deck. Previous profiles of the businessman, from Mencken to Galbraith, associate him with the hangman and the scavenger and make him the uncultured brute that revels in private affluence and causes public squalor. True, he shares these properties with other socially accepted rogues: bandits, tort lawyers, and slumlords, all of whom argue for the sovereignty of private means over public ends. But while these rapscallions have been portrayed in books and even in blockbuster pictures, from *The Firm* to *The Sopranos* and Michael Moore's movies, corporate characters have never been featured as representatives of a well-defined third culture.

This collection is not intended as the businessman's apotheosis. Neither will you read an apology for his deeds, nor an outright condemnation of his attitudes. As Arthur Miller said about Willy Loman, "He's not the finest character that ever lived." That is true; but he is also not the worst. Navigating his ambivalent morality has prevented him from ever being really evil or truly good, outrageously funny or shockingly silly. The world of business is largely an irony-free zone. Countering this sorry state of corporate humor, I have, in describing this world, used many literary tropes, such as analogy, simile, metaphor, parody, caricature and even slapstick, all meant to paint an intrinsically gray terrain in brighter colors.

"It seems," wrote Isaac Bashevis Singer, "that the analysis of character is the highest human entertainment. And literature does it, unlike gossip, without mentioning real names." Therefore, no businessman will be mentioned by name, unless it was necessary for the plot or the joke I wanted to make.

I
Elementary Characters

The Chief Executive Officer, or CEO

The CEO shares with the Pope the gift of infallibility, and with Moses the certainty that his corporate objectives, a.k.a. commandments, are of a divine origin. He commands a posse of cardinals and bishops, his vice presidents. They make up his cabinet, they have a *portefeuille*, a post and responsibilities, and they believe in the motto that the Marquis de Lafayette lived by: "Think little, but firmly!"

The CEO, however, must think much, and he must think big.

Money is the first item within the categories of "much" and "big." There is a sign on the CEO's desk that says, "The Buck Stops Here." This defiant instruction may seem like a sly reference to the dog named Buck in Jack London's *Call of the Wild*, who, as everyone remembers, becomes (at the end of the book) the pack's alpha

17

wolf. More likely, though, it hints at the CEO's pay: Hardly a dollar shall pass beyond this desk without a part of it being pocketed by him. Indeed, the salary of a CEO is usually given in six figures or more, while his philosophy can be expressed in only six words. They were written in a letter by the Roman philosopher Seneca (4 BC – 65 AD) to his friend Lucilius:

Cum ad summum perveneris, paria sunt.

When you are at the summit, everybody else looks equal.

Or in the CEO's own vernacular:

To the top dog everybody else is just a dog.

Alpha comes before Beta and Gamma. Looking from his corner office down upon the masses of Beta directors and managers and Gamma employees toiling in cubicles, he can see that some of them are more unequal than others. How many lives of unequals depend on him? He roughly knows, but doesn't care. In this, he follows the poet Ovid (43 BC – 18 AD), who wrote that numbers are only for the pauper:

Pauperis est numerare pecus.

Only the poor man counts his cattle.

The pay for the employed cattle, properly called their *pecuniary* reward (from *pecus* – cattle), is only a skinny fraction of the CEO's, by a factor of 10 or 50. That's because they are remunerated for their work only, and as "at will" employees they can be severed from the company for cause or without rhyme or reason. By comparison, the CEO, who doesn't labor but lead, has a fat severance package, which is, in legal terms, his prenup with the company as his bride.

In his free time he plays golf (a double-digit handicap, in spite of multiple Mulligans), and on Saturday nights he sometimes accompanies his wife to the symphonic orchestra, for which they have season tickets. He is, in his own words, "very open to good music."

His favorites include Mozart's "Night Serenade" and Johann Strauss Jr.'s "Emperor's Waltz." From his days of courtship he also remembers Maurice Ravel's "Bolero," but he is not sure anymore in which context those pulsing rhythms once seemed relevant. Of American music he cherishes most Aaron Copeland's *Rodeo*, "Buckeroo Holiday" being his absolute favorite, because they always play it at his Equestrian Club. During the day he sometimes taps his fingers to Muzak's elevator music. That, for him, is a successful distillation of tonal happiness wrapped in non-threatening arrangements. Once he read in the *Wall Street Journal* that Muzak (together with Andy Warhol's cans of Campbell soup) is our post-industrial life's most authentic art form, because it is endlessly repeatable and non-offensive. Whatever the pundits say, it calms him down.

Buying two outrageously expensive glasses of champagne during intermission shows the CEO's cultural commitment to the arts, and a plaque in the lobby of the Symphony Hall is proof of his responsibilities as a corporate sponsor and benefactor of cultural causes. He generously admits that he is not a specialist in music or art. No, he has no critical opinion about Wyeth's "Helga" pictures, for instance. But, personally, he likes her blond and naive nakedness. Yes, he certainly knows what he likes.

His PR department realizes how important it is that the CEO will be seen during the correct fund raising events. The Science Center and the Opera House are great photo opportunities, United Way campaigns and Retirement Home openings are OK. Pro Choice events, Aids Awareness rallies, and Gay Pride parades are definite no-no's. He prefers to read about these controversial gatherings in the safe, square, and self-confident prose of the *Wall Street Journal*.

Since graduating from Business School he has been a conservative, staunch in the defense of tax breaks, but less dogmatic with regards to environmental policy loopholes. He owns a gun (but has never used it) – for him it's a matter of principle in support of the Second Amendment. Justices and judges, he says, should be umpires and never pitch or bat. He has voted Republican since his second year in college, but Trump makes him uncomfortable. He has said he would never employ Ted Cruz, because he would give our customers the creeps.

The Hands-On

The Hands-On has narrow vision, which he calls focus. Just like his idol, the legendary steel-driver John Henry, he comes down heavily on things with his hammer and prefers to touch his objects with his own hands rather than use fancy technology, or think about anything in abstract terms. When in a reflective mood, the Hands-On calls himself a hard-core realist. He looks down on co-workers who make plans before they act. He calls them "fuzzy thinkers". He laughs at those who write wussy specifications before they compose software.

He lives what he preaches. He owns a sturdy four-wheel drive, which he repairs himself (even when it isn't broken). His wife's hair is short and straight (the way he likes it), and she doesn't wear make-up. He insists, however, on a dab of aftershave for himself before taking her to their bowling night on Friday.

Back at work he strives to be known as a "doer." When somebody talks about the weather, that it is too warm for a bike-ride, or too cold to go fishing, or too rainy for anything, then he's the one who'll say "let's do something about it." And he does. He taps on the barometer, shakes the thermometer, and looks threateningly towards the sky. This can-do attitude is an indication that for a Hands-On nothing is considered impossible, some things, as he likes to say, " just take a little longer," and most things don't make sense anyway.

For the Hands-On, finishing a project is more exciting than starting it, or working on it. For him, the way is not the reward, and when he tinkers (which he always does), his pectorals are more involved than his frontal lobe, and his sweat glands more than his pineal gland. If he were educated and had read Pascal (which he wouldn't because Pascal was a mystic and a fuzzy thinker), he would have heard about the *esprit de géométrie* and the *esprit de finesse*. Being matter-of-fact he'll identify with the straightforward,

rectangular, ungirlish geometrical spirit and look at the sense of finesse as if it were a whimsical piece of lingerie.

The Hands-On is a crude personification of Benjamin Franklin's
definition of man as a toolmaker, who for Marx represented the
very characteristics of "Yankeedom," that is, of the modern age and
thus of corporate life. Yet the Hands-On is also Emerson's true
American Scholar. "I ask not for the great," the Hands-on reads in
that famous essay (with which he agrees), "the remote, the roman-
tic. (…) I embrace the common, I explore and sit at the feet of the
familiar, the low. Give me insight into today, and you may have
the antique and future worlds. What would we really know the
meaning of? The meal in the firkin; the milk in the pan; the ballad
in the street; the news of the boat; the glance of the eye; the form
and the gait of the body; (…) there is no trifle, there is no puzzle,
but one design unites and animates the farthest pinnacle and the
lowest trench."

The Fussbudget

Limited in size and valid only for a fixed period of time, a budget records the size of the critical resources targeted for a particular purpose. Adding "fuss" turns a budget into a Fussbudget. The Fussbudget, however, has resources that are unlimited and available to him at any time, useful for no purpose other than fuss, fuss, fuss.

Different from the Nitpicker, who focuses his criticism on selected, if extraneous, details, the Fussbudget spreads his fastidious attention over several miscellaneous issues large and small about which he worries especially at times when everything is going well, complains about when everybody is happy, and protests against when everything has already been decided. The Nitpicker picks locally, at his favorite locations only, and one nit at a time. The Fussbudget fusses globally, wherever his general discomforts and specific displeasures pique him, and all at the same time.

These activities create a level of irrational heat sufficient to warm a four-person household. Defying such utilitarian thoughts, however, the Fussbudget prefers to provide hot air only to increase the entropy of the entire system surrounding him. With this carefree application of thermodynamic laws, he can successfully diffuse his energies and add to the general disorder until a state of chaos has been safely reached. Then, finally, the Fussbudget feels comfortable.

Most comfortable for a Fussbudget is a life in the city of Pidneres. You do not know Pidneres? But you certainly know the famous oriental habitat of Serendip, where one finds valuable or agreeable things not sought for – serendipities. Pidneres is its sister city in the occidental hemisphere, where every citizen indulges in the habit of seeking invaluable and disagreeable things, and he finds them! Once found, he pays very close attention to them, turning them over and over in his hands and in his mind as if they were the most precious bugaboos, uncovering new facets to agitate about and new angles to excite him – all of which reinforces his utter fascination with things gone wrong.

Thus the Fussbudget has brought us a creative and disturbing reworking of Murphy's Law. He is disappointed when something that can go wrong doesn't go wrong. He has warped the Peter Principle into a new corporate wisdom, to wit: In a hierarchy every Fussbudget tends to rise to a level where his fussiness proves his incompetence. The Fussbudget has even upset Parkinson's Law: His work expands into fuss so that there is never enough time available to complete it.

A Shakespearean quote explains why the Fussbudget likes to surround himself lovingly with the clang and clatter of persnickety trivialities: It is the empty vessel, Shakespeare writes, that makes the loudest sound.

The Nitpicker

When it is small it interests him, when it is insignificant he seriously objects to it, and everything that is minuscule excites him beyond reason.

Making the small and insignificant nit a matter of great importance is his whole concern, and succeeding once again in the megalomania of the mini quibble gives him superior job satisfaction. Happiness for him comes from the challenges that lie in the hitherto undisputed detail - if indeed happiness it is. For happiness is rather a large sentiment for his myopic yet quarrelsome mind. He prefers his microscopic rewards in a sequence of tiny victories, strung together like the beads on the rosary of his childhood.

Since his cradle days he has always insisted on his right to complain, from the composition of the baby milk formula to his quantum of spinach at lunch as a schoolboy. As as a young man he counted the leaves on trees (and said he was missing some) when everybody else was rhapsodizing about the beauty of the forest. Now, as a grown-up, he is an expert on the rules of limitations and exceptions, insisting on the unalienable right to contradict a majority opinion, or dispute that the law of averages works: that a particular outcome or event is inevitable because, on average, it *has* happened in the past. But not to me, he says. He looks for flaws in perfection, and if he cannot find them he creates them by insisting stubbornly that flaws do exist and he has seen them before.

Eventually he becomes the Master Of The Marginal, chief of the feared order of Fanatics for Criticism of Minutiae. Their members are in charge of the pedantic police-work of watching over the crossing of t's and dotting of i's.

In discussions the Nitpicker plays his cherished role of tetrapyloctomist, the artist of splitting hair four different ways. When his department plans for budgets and next year's strategies, he is tired and inclined to gloss over the big picture, only to come alive ferociously to fight for, or attack, the allotment for the purchase of thumbtacks.

His most fastidious ways show in his own office. His pencils are sharpened, although never used. Every evening, exactly at five o'-clock, he cleans each key of his keyboard with a q-tip, five keys per q-tip, using twenty of them every day.

The Empty Suit

Years ago, in an act of comic iconoclasm, Garry Trudeau, creator of Doonesbury, began to represent certain well-known public figures as icons. The first icon was a "point o' lite" for George H.W. "Poppy" Bush. Drawn as an empty space, the point o' lite was an eloquent oxymoron: a visible void, a distinctive nil, a full-fledged nothing. Even wrapped in the business outfit of an heir to oil wells, or clad in the baseball uniform of a Yalie, such a Void Persona is, in TexSpeak, "All hat and no cattle," or, in CorpSpeak, an Empty Suit.

The Empty Suit is the complement to the Emperor wearing his New Clothes: the latter was a man without clothes, the former is clothes without a man. Instead of a child saying, "But Mommy, he's naked!" corporate employees whisper, "That suit is Smith from Marketing. He acts like hot stuff, but he's empty." Or, "That's Carly over there by the Lear Jet. Boy, is she an empty suit!" Others, including Hewlett-Packard employees who've read *Catcher in the Rye*, use another synonym for an Empty Suit: "She's a phony."

Our American culture has given us many fine examples for the old Latin saying *vestis virum facit* – "clothes make the man," from Clark Kent in Superman's outfit to Bruce Wayne's Batman suit. Just as these gentlemen slip into their leotards, the Empty Suit dons his Jos. A. Bank or Armani disguise to become a different being every morning. However, the Empty Suit does not spend his workday by saving Gotham. He merely *acts as if* he is about to save Gotham. During critical situations of serious customer complaints against his department, he is the first to address the problem (which he calls "a welcome challenge") by declaring that it is no longer enough to talk about customer support or customer service. Even customer "care" doesn't describe what he wants to say. "We must be willing to take the extra step and *delight* our customers!" With this meaningless directive and a hand wave indicating that the "welcome challenge" has now been delegated to his team, he leaves for another meeting, while the sweet and icky smell of the word "delight" stays behind as a reminder of the Empty Suit.

The Empty-Suit shines in meetings. Not like a candle in the night; his dim intellect produces only about 15 Watts. Not like a spotlight on stage either; he prefers not to focus on any topic, but to diffuse every issue with his tedious wordiness. Least of all is he like a beacon in a lighthouse. The light he gives off rather resembles the ashen remnants of crumpled newspapers smoldering in a trashcan. Think William "Bill" Lumbergh from the movie "Office Space." Yet everybody notices the white gleam coming off his starched shirt cuffs, and the sheen from his self-satisfied cheeks.

But it isn't the garment or his aftershave alone that makes an Empty Suit. More often it is the emptiness inside. The Empty Suit favors hierarchy over participation, formality over warmth, uniformity over diversity. He usually knows what the boss wants, so he sells himself upward. But since his personality – what there is of it – rubs even the top brass wrong at times, he doesn't breeze through the ranks as easily as the Fair-Haired Boy. The Empty Suit develops his own professional craft of polishing his Italian shoes, his overhead slides, his language, and his boss's apple.

The successful Empty-Suit apple polisher will eventually climb to the rank of high-patina Empty Executive Suit. Having gone to the right B-School helps: it adds glamour, certification, and - sooner or later - a higher salary. While other students from his graduating class were idealistically looking at a full life on an empty stomach, he decided on an empty suit with a full wallet. All he has to do now, day after day, is dress for success.

At night at home he peels off his Armani cloak and becomes a Nothing. It is rumored that in the morning his bed looks like nobody slept in it.

The Fair-Haired Boy

He can do no wrong, however hard he tries – which he doesn't. Whether it is his lucky star, his benevolent mentor, or his pleasant looks, his good fortune can be explained even less than it can be in doubt. He is like an effect without a cause. He is a result beyond reason. He defies gravity by always falling upstairs.

The Fair-Haired Boy is not an expert in his field, but he does have talent. As a precocious youngster he often showed some striking abilities, such as playing the piano with cute seriousness, in the manner Schroeder of the Peanuts comic strip plays Beethoven. Since he is oblivious to standards by which normal mortals are measured, he maintains a sense of independence, which doesn't turn him into a revolutionary, but it does boost his popularity. Famous examples of such independent talents are Linus Torvalds, the inventor of the Linux kernel and darling of the open source software community, the young Leo di Caprio, and the former Bayern soccer star Philipp Lahm.

In a corporation, the Fair-Haired Boy enjoys his blissful life from little success to bigger promotion, winning praise and merit and higher pay on the way. The seemingly innocent light of his sometimes unearned, but never undeserved successes shines brighter than the eyes of a Lottery winner. An all-American golden boy, his smile is the trademark of suburban Camelot. He may have been a fashion model for Ralph Lauren in his teens. He doesn't pretend to be omniscient. He is not a genius, but genial and intelligent. Think CNN news anchor Cooper Anderson.

Sport franchises like to brag about their power players, such as Alex "A-Rod" Rodriguez of the Yankees. But players like him are too ambitious and professional, they have too much testosterone, or are prettied up to become superstars and models (like David Beckham). The true Fair-Haired Boy doesn't turn Alpha-male or sissy boy, but remains an amateur with an innocent matinee idol quality on a small stage. We like the junior college quarterback because he takes no brassy credit for his wins and no blame for his losses. He shows no exaggerated cleverness or wit. He has no blemishes either, no sharp edges on his face or his temperament. His personality has been well-rounded by the constant stream of random luck and sweet success, like water rounding a pebble in a brook. Think about the young, blond, and handsome John Elway when he played football at Stanford, or Joseph, favorite son of Jacob and Rachel (see Genesis 37).

Even a Fair-Haired Boy can make a fool of himself, and then his gleam proves to be fool's gold and mere patina. A false-shining example was Paul Hornung of the Green Bay Packers, friend of the ladies and the Rich and Famous. He was suspended for gambling and then wrote a pathetic book about his fall with the title *Golden Boy*, subtitled "Girls, Games, and Gambling at Green Bay." Another example: Mark Hurd, former CEO of HP, was for five years the golden boy of Wall Street (and simultaneously the anti-Christ for HP employees). Through rather petty scandals, he fell into a self-made well of embarrassment, which was however softened by a $40 million severance pay cushion and a big job with Oracle.

Other Fair-Haired Boys, who were less shallow than Horning or Hurd, met their fate in a more dramatic and memorable way. Take Shakespeare's golden boy Hamlet. As the Danish crown prince he must have looked a lot like John Elway, playing catch with his friends Rosencrantz and Guildenstern. But then, with the ghostly knowledge that his father was murdered by his uncle Claudius, who had meanwhile married his widowed mother, and with the added aggravation of falling madly in love with Ophelia, Hamlet turned from slender Fair-Haired-Boy to clumsy killer of Polonius and shilly-shally monologist, who didn't do sports anymore, so that his mother Gertrude called him "fat and scant of breath."

Another example where the sweetness of a golden boy turned sour was recorded by Homer. Achilles, the Greek Fair-Haired Boy, threw a tantrum in the camp before Troy when King Agamemnon, citing royal privileges, took the lovely girl Briseis from him. As is well known, Achilles pouted and refused to lead his troops alongside the other Greek forces. Only after the Trojan general Hector had killed Achilles' friend Patroclus did Achilles get his mojo back and revenged Patroclus by chasing Hector around Troy, finally killing him in a duel, and afterwards dragging his corpse around the walls of Troy for nine full days. The moral of this tale: Don't take from a Fair-Haired Boy what he thinks is rightfully his, or his vanity will turn into rages of senseless cruelty.

Perhaps the most moving example of a Fair-Haired-Boy's tragic fall from grace, like an angel dropping from heaven, is the hapless and beloved sailor Billy Budd in Melville's novel, "the young fellow who seems so popular with the men – Billy, the Handsome Sailor," as his Captain Vere calls him. Harassed and accused unjustly of mutiny by the evil John Cloggart, Billy strikes out and accidentally kills him. For this deed he must hang. Such is the law, but it is not justice, and Captain Vere regretfully summarizes the fates of the bully Cloggart and Fair-Haired Billy: "Struck dead by an angel of God! Yet the angel must hang!"

The Godfather

Almost anybody can work. Some even like it. But only a handful of us enjoy the *succes fou* of making mad money, becoming made men, and winning glory. To achieve all that, you need a Godfather.

In a corporation, as in any *cosa nostra*, a Godfather derives his power from the loyalty of his clan, the hatred of his enemies, and his connections beyond friends and foes. "Keep your friends close, but keep your enemies closer," is his motto. Hence, for you to make it as a fellow Mafioso and to "become a made man," you too must love and protect his family, know and hate his enemies, and benefit from his connections. Membership in his clan (project team, department, division) is not free. You have to be worthy. You have to pay with the shekels of your soul and the lifeblood of your career. Then you will – perhaps – rise with him; and – certainly – fall when he does.

The Godfather plays three roles for which the Italian language has the names *padre, padrino,* and *padrone* – that is: father, godfather, and godlike boss, the *capo di tutti capi.* First, he is the *padre* to his close family, the father who provides protection and provisions, expecting respect and obedience in return. Second, he is the *padrino* to the larger clan of adopted friends like you, the godfather who'll keep an eye on you from afar when things are going well, and from close up when you are in trouble. You pay in advance with your loyalty by being a runner for the family and an information carrier for the clan. And third, he is the *padrone* to everybody, the master of fate, the boss over people, the lord over life.

In the old days, the role of the *padrone* also included the obligation to be a patron of the arts, as Gaius Maecenas was for Horace and his risky poetry. Maecenas held the unofficial post of minister of culture for a competing, much more powerful Godfather, the divine *mafioso* known in history books as Emperor Augustus, who wanted to hire professionals like Horace as secretary in their own cadre of god-children. But Horace was not handsome enough for Augustus to escalate the issue with Maecenas, who owned Horace at the time. Horace's younger colleague Ovid got himself into deeper trouble with the same *padrone* Augustus. Having seen something "unspeakable" in or around Augustus' palace (the exact nature of the "unspeakable" has remained unknown to this day) Ovid was sent on a long business trip to Tomi at the shores of the Black Sea without a return ticket. His story shows that falling from grace is much quicker than rising in your Godfather's favor.

Later Godfathers have included patriarchs and popes, patricians from the Fuggers to the Rockefellers, vice-presidents of companies and football clubs. All are representatives of feudal power outside the principles of democratic control. Even the supposed guardians of democracy, unions or congress or media conglomerates, have their gangs and capos.

Vito Corleone has many fans and remains the prototype of the modern Godfather who owns people's loyalty and manipulates them for his own good, making offers so persuasive that no one can refuse. Today's Godfathers are permitted to complement persuasion with legal guns, thanks to the late Supreme Court Justice Antonin Scalia, who in the 2008 case *District of Columbia v. Heller* held that the word "militia" in the Second Amendment meant, originally, "the body of all citizens," and that therefore the right to bear arms was never meant exclusively for guns in a military context, but happily permits individual gun ownership to any Godfather. Rupert Murdoch of Fox News, another *padrone*, doesn't require fire arms, because he has hired guns like Sean Hannity and the silly puppets of Fox and Friends.

Information from your Godfather's network of connections with friends and foes can obviously be good for your career. You will learn about better jobs in advance, you will have access to unpublished org-charts, and your merits, together with your availability, can be trumpeted through the channels of this communication web. On the other hand, what you learn from having near total access can be disillusioning. You may learn that your favorite general manager sacrificed a marketing manager to save his own scalp; that the admired lab manager with his thirty patents is a womanizing sleaze bag; that you are on a vice president's hit list; and that your Godfather hasn't even said good-bye when he left the company this morning to work for the competition.

The Curmudgeon

Theophrastus, in his 22nd character sketch, outlined the features of the Curmudgeon that walked the halls of his institute of philosophy in Athens with the same gait and facial expression as we see him today in the hallways of Corporate America.

While concentrating almost exclusively on the Curmudgeon as a money-grabbing, penny-pinching, ill-tempered miser, Theophrastus also wants his readers to understand the most serious limitations of this pathetic character. By calling him "aneleuteros", which means "not free," he is, according to the Greeks not a full-fledged citizen. Theophrastus emphasizes that the Curmudgeon's behavior and principles are unworthy of a true human being.

Some three-hundred years later, Horace also has harsh words about this miserly character. In his book on Poetics he writes about the Curmudgeon as a stage character. He describes him as an avaricious boor, a wintry man, cantankerous and crotchety, a critic of youth, and full of praise for the good old days.

A similar sentiment was reported already by Homer in 800 B.C. In the Iliad, we hear about the Curmudgeons sitting on top of the tall Skaian gate, the main entrance to the city of Troy. Too old, too feeble, or too cowardly to hurl a lance at the Greeks, they are perched on their high seats like cicadas on trees, commenting on everything in their thin "delicate voice of singing." Smacking their lips like old geezers they gush over the incredibly beautiful Helen, but what with their dried-up loins and inability to compete with the godlike hulk Paris, they would rather she went home to her lawful hubby Menelaos than cause more "grief to us and our children."

Like his cousin, the Has-Been, the Curmudgeon lives without a future. Hence his most distinctive feature: his bull-headed and occasionally red-necked resentment and backwardness. You will hardly find the likes of him in R&D or Marketing departments, but rather more often in staff functions on Corporate Hill, or Finance. Occasionally you may still detect these descendants of the Trojan aldermen deep in the groves of manufacturing where obsolete widgets are made.

Crusty with the self-righteous indignation that is prevalent also in his brother, the Know-It-All, the Curmudgeon will resist change even after it has swept over him. Not only has he seen it all: a Curmudgeon was once overheard grumbling, while glancing over Michelangelo's ceiling in the Sistine Chapel: "Is that it?"

The Has-Been

The Has-Been flaunts a defensive look of nostalgia and defiance. A proud plaque on his desk and a complimentary letter from management (kept in his drawer) are distant reminders of the seven years that were fat and satisfying. Having maintained a certain reputation of experience, reliability, and caution, he is useful when given no-risk assignments and projects that have predictable outcomes. In his daily work he now follows the principle of not trying his darndest when his next-to-darndest will do. On a performance scale from 1 to 5 his managers rate him a 3.

Years back, when the company faced many challenges, he took his chances. He was promoted and he supervised his own team for seven good years. Then one day, after many nights of overtime and sacrifice, followed by two or three promotions and some riskier jobs, he began to make mistakes, an error of judgment here, a missed deadline there. Was he in over his head? His peers thought so. His managers agreed. Whether it was his fault or not, it was him who was blamed. He was not skilled at defense. He pouted, withdrew, was angry, and talked back. After a serious talk with representatives from HR, he maintained his pay level but lost his team. Unmotivated to start anew and not wanting to leave the company (because of the stock purchase plan, reasonably good health insurance, a short drive to work), he ended up first in quality control, then in customer service. The drift towards mediocrity became his only direction. He resigned himself, but he never resigned from his company. In the years following, still a respected veteran, a loyal, reliable employee, he received a memorial watch, recovered his spirits at least partly and was generally seen as a well of knowledge, if not exactly a fountain of new ideas.

Alone in his cubicle with not much to do, he continues to chew on his memories like a cow on her cud. He mulls over the past and ruminates about what could have been. He never thinks about the future, because he knows he has none, because there's no comeback for a Has-Been. Or is there?

In those shilly-shally moments mixed of hope and doubt, he admits to himself that Has-Beens are not born – they are made, mostly self-made. So perhaps F. Scott Fitzgerald was not right when he wrote there are no second acts in American families? If you look around, he tells himself, there's for instance Nixon, who lost in 1960 to Kennedy and came back in 1968 – but then fell, impeached and disgraced, rather deeply. Warren Beatty recovered after "Ishtar" and made "Dick Tracy" and "Bugsy" and "Bulworth." But then flopped again with "Town and Country." For a Has-Been, the vacillations in life don't follow an iambic down-up, down-up rhythm, they drum along in dreary and ominous up-down, up-down trochees.

At this point in his musings he plays the old and faded VHS cassette with the movie "They never come back" and clenches his fists when come-back kid Jimmy Nolan (played by Regis Toomey) wins his last fight and $1,000 against all odds. He mutters to himself that Cassius Clay also came back as the even better boxer Muhammad Ali. And that Has-Been actor Ronald Reagan came back as President of the United States. Many say that in this highest office Reagan performed still like an actor, and as far as presidential acting goes was more convincing than what he had shown for instance as George "The Gipper" Gipp and as the double amputee in "Kings Row," where his most famous line was "Where's the rest of me?"

This is also the problem for the Has-Been: "Where's the rest of me, the rest of my life?" It's down in the valley of despair, and only the most astute of the Has-Beens will realize that he has become just like Paul Bunyan's Goofus Bird, which builds its nest upside down and flies backward, not caring where it is going, only where it has been.

The Corporate Gentleman

The Corporate Gentleman holds a distinguished position within the company, and he broadcasts the corresponding pose of refinement and dress-for-success dignity into his surroundings. It is a mystery what his exact position is or was. He was once important, in a way nobody seems to remember, and he still reports to the vice president of sales. His business card says "Senior Corporate Fellow". He has no direct reports and must therefore think and talk for himself. Two or three times a year, he accompanies his vice president on a trip to a so-called "customer facing event", where he always "makes a very good impression" and "represents the corporation exceptionally well", as his performance evaluation tells us. His demeanor of self-importance, signaled by a silk tie and a Three-piece-suit by Boss, overshadows his words, and his manners are more noticeable than his actions. He is still young, or at least not old. His ageless poise seems to convey an authoritative air of seniority and timeless sovereignty that you challenge at your own risk. He may be the inventor of the infamous "TPS report" starring in the movie "Office Space."

His facial expression is festive, yet he never seems to celebrate. *Prim* is too small a word for him, just as *civilized* is too pretentious, and *educated* somehow doesn't come to mind. One has to settle on "gentlemanly." On the other hand, there remains an undeniable suggestion of sweetness, however faint, as from a perfumed cigar, in the atmosphere when he has passed, not the animal smell of power or money. No speck of dust spoils the shine on his shoes, no grit of corporate muscle hardens his clean-shaven chin. The epithet of smoothness fits him like a silken glove. He has a Faulknerian languor and speaks Business-School language as if it were a foreign tongue to him. His face is Clark Gable's, minus the masculinity. His gestures are debonair, without the classy flair of an elegant rogue. In an orchestra, he wouldn't be concert master; he matches the third chair in the viola section where he doesn't play many notes but is still very much visible to the audience.

Since he is a Gentleman, it is not his style to suggest, let alone use brute force, professional skills, or specialized knowledge to solve a problem. Instead of solving a problem, he prefers to raise a small but pertinent issue carefully, addressing it from afar, perhaps reformulating it, and then politely suggesting "that someone should take it from here." This may take three years. Amiable and aloof, he shuns confrontations and prefers honorable retreat over competition or contradiction. His ways are indirect, his methods oblique, his manners and shirts impeccable, his phrases inoffensive. These attributes are enough to give him the upper hand when nobody else cares to fight and win. When he is tired, he looks more like a Mafioso's third son who was often sick as a child and who wanted to become a cardinal or bishop, but ended up as minister in a corporation. He collects things that are more precious than valuable. He is Walter Benjamin's "Etui-Man": "the Etui-Man looks for comfort, of which the case (the *etui*) is the quintessence." The Corporate Gentleman lives inside this case of comfort.

His weakness? He mistakes gravitas for importance, polite chat for wit, self-importance for self-awareness. When, at the end of the day, he gets tired of being a gentleman, he may turn stuffy. Umberto Eco's Piemontese character Belpo would mutter to him, "Ma gavte la nata," which means: "Take the cork out, man, and let the wind break."

The Busybody

[A contribution by Theophrastus]

What the Busybody offers is done out of some affected, artificial kindness, not because his contribution is of much use. In a project he will take on a part that greatly exceeds his ability. After a critical point has been settled to the satisfaction of all, he will pipe up and insist on some trivial objection.

At banquets he argues with the waiter and asks for more liquor than the guests can possibly consume. He interferes in quarrels between parties of whom he knows nothing. He offers to be the guide in a walk through a forest, loses his way immediately and is forced to confess that he knows nothing about where to go. He will interrupt a vice president's talk to his team and inquire what the strategy is going to be. Or ask what directives the vice president will give out tomorrow.

He is wont to give his father information about his mother's movements. Although the physician has forbidden wine to his patient, the Busybody will, nevertheless, give him some, just to see – so he says – what will happen.

When his wife dies, he inscribes on her tombstone not only her name and good qualities as a wife, but also those of her husband, father, and mother, adding: "They were all people of extraordinary virtue." As a witness in court, taking an oath, he cannot withstand the temptation of informing everyone around him that it is not the first time he has been asked to give evidence.

[Note: This corporate character "The Busybody", was (freely) translated from Theophrastus' seventh character Peri Periergias. The verb periergazomai means "to insert oneself in other peoples' affairs", and the noun periergia means "overdone care about details and fussiness." To add more etymological detail, ergon is "work", "action" or "effort" in a rather general sense, and with peri + genitive meaning here "regarding" and

"about" and *"around"* (see periphery), periergia nicely captures the characteristics of somebody *"futzing about the work activities of others,"* which describes the Busybody. Some phrases in the translation above were taken from Francis Howell's translation, published by Josiah Taylor, Architectural Library, London, 1824.]

The Personnel Director

Etymologically, the Personnel Director derives his job title from the word *persona*, the Latin noun for mask, and from *dirigo, direxi, directus*, a verb meaning straighten out someone or something, to bring and keep things and people in line (as explained in the Employee Handbook). These people exist primarily through their submitted resumes, which serve as masks behind which every employee can hide just like an actor in a play. It is possible that Byron, in his canto xi, stanza 37, was thinking of his resume when he was writing

And, after all, what is a lie? 'Tis but
The truth in masquerade.

Today, the term "personnel" is more often associated with lowly maids and cooks entering smelly kitchens through basement delivery entrances. Traditionally, as we know from the soap opera "Downton Abbey," personnel is called "staff" that live and work downstairs, while the master resides upstairs. To avoid such a parallel between maids (down) and master (up), employees (down) and employer (up), the Personnel Director has been renamed the Head of Human Resources HR, which has a fuller, more humane sound. Calling the dealings with personnel a matter of Human Resources is also more honest, because it refers to humans not as *servants* like maids, i.e., people (no matter how insignificant), but instead as *material production resources* on par with wood and bricks and water pumps. And just as wood and bricks and water pumps are neatly collected in sheds and warehouses, where they are stored and inventoried for ready use, so are the employee resources collected in cubicles with alphabetical files stored on a computer in the HR Director's office.

Little wonder then that the computerized HR Director encounters corporate citizens mainly in the reduced form of data. While formerly there existed a full-fledged body, often with a soul attached, standing in front of him and asking for information about the new benefits package, now there is just an Excel spreadsheet, with color-coded notes that tell him at a glance how to read employee Betty's dossier: What is her employee number? Is she exempt? Is she a member of a union? What is her performance rating? How many times has Betty complained about her manager?

Once or twice a year, the HR Director meets employees in the flesh, most likely at the occasion of the New Employee Orientation assembly. Standing on a podium, at a safe distance from the freshly arrived resources, he looks like a thoroughly amiable fellow, tells everybody to call him Al, and indeed he looks like Paul Simon's Al, the one from "Why am I soft in the middle? The rest of my life is so hard!" Employee Handbook in hand, he'll talk for two hours about your complete benefit package, the advantage of flex time, casual dress Fridays, teamwork, and that – if you work hard – you will for a long time be part of "something great." If the company were a family, as his words suggest, then he would not only be employee Betty's friend Al but her mother, father, uncle, brother, and sister: "For any issue, however small or big, I will be there for you:

> I can be your long lost pal!
> I can call you Betty,
> And Betty, when you call me,
> You can call me Al!"

Such an overly generous invitation to share your corporate pain and open your hearts to the Personnel Director and Head of HR calls for skepticism and caution. Here are two common scenarios to be aware of.

(1) When you have any issue at your job that you cannot solve by yourself, for instance a conflict with a fellow employee, ask your manager to work with you at a resolution. Never count on the Personnel Director as the referee in serious matters, regardless of how petty the cause of your conflict appears, or how small or big the is-

sue is that makes you angry or unhappy. All you'll receive is a secret mark in your personnel file.

(2) One of the worst tactical mistakes an employee can make is to believe the Personnel Director is his or her friend and ally in a serious disagreement with a manager of the company. The Personnel Director is not an Ombudsman, and he'll never act as your advocate against the company and its leadership.

In the language of maids and master, the Personnel Director is the master's butler who occasionally visits downstairs, but he works upstairs, and that's where his loyalties are.

The Corporate Counsel

The man in the street and the peasant in the field both agree with Shakespeare's scoundrel Dick from Jack Cade's gang in Henry IV (2), Act 4, scene 2. Dick said:

"The first thing we do, let's kill all the lawyers."

But, of course, nobody would dare even injure a lawyer by, say, running a bicycle over his legs. The continuing bloom of tort cases – the lawful art of turning personal injury into profit – is a scary phenomenon for the easily inhibited, be they man, peasant, or biker. Killing him, however justified, may lead to criminal charges. But mocking a lawyer seems safe.

Magnus Oleson was one of the quiet Norwegian peasants and forebears of the people at Garrison Keillor's Lake Wobegon. His contempt for bankers was only surpassed by his disdain for lawyers, and after many dealings with the latter, he put his accumulated derision into a farmer's language. "Honesty in a lawyer," he said, "is like a hen's hind legs." This rural simile, not easy to understand by people living in cities, is First Amendment free speech and not considered enough to warrant serious litigation for slander.

The joy of litigation was bequeathed to all of us in the cradle by the evil witch. It was wrapped together with the gifts of prejudice and malice. Thus every peasant has a lawyer inside of him as his alter ego or, as Freud may have diagnosed, as the uncontrollable force of the id, which can be defined as a deep power behind the human drive for sex, money, and justice (as a lawyer sees it).

Conversely, every lawyer carries a peasant inside because he, the lawyer, also wants to harvest more in autumn than he has sown in spring.

Which brings us to the lawyer in a corporation, the Corporate Counsel. Since the Godfather movies with Marlon Brando, Al Pacino, and the rest of the Corleone family, Robert Duvall's cool consigliere Tom Hagen has become the model for every Corporate Counsel. What a godfather, or a CEO, may simply call loyalty to the family and corporation, the Corporate Counsel puts more formally to words as follows:

> It shall be the duty of an advocate fearlessly to uphold the interests of his client by all fair and honorable means without regard to any unpleasant consequences to himself or any other. He shall defend a person accused of a crime regardless of his personal opinion as to the guilt of the accused, bearing in mind that his loyalty is to the law and to the corporation.

In more practical terms, a Corporate Counsel's duties are at once defensive and aggressive. In his defensive role he must protect the corporation against possible suits by employees. Examples include (allegedly unfair) rightsizing, sexual and other harassment, disputes over rights of stock options and other perks. In these cases, which have rarely been won by employees, the Corporate Counsel works closely together with the Ombudsman and Human Resources. When the competition of his company becomes too successful, or if a company patent is being infringed upon, or if a newspaper becomes too critical, then he needs to turn aggressive and "go after" the adversaries.

There is one more task that calls upon both his aggressive and defensive nature. In concert with bankers, the Corporate Counsel either prepares a takeover of another company, or he prepares the defense of a takeover launched by his legal peers from another company. In no known case are the welfare of the employees, or the productivity of the company, or the benefit for the economy at large, in the center of this frantic game of boardroom monopoly by lawyers and bankers. No; in these dual roles the consigliere has finally interpreted Magnus Oleson's verdict in his own favor. The reference to a hen's woebegone legs is a meme for the Corporate

Counsel's intention to feather his nest, acquire a golden nest egg and continue, in his role as Beelezebub, with his godlike CEO "hatching his vain empires" (after Milton's "Paradise Lost", Book 2).

The Executive Secretary

"Buxom, blithe, and debonair," so Milton writes in his poem "L'Allegro," the Executive Secretary is dressed in a high-efficiency business-suit with a high-collared blouse consistent with her elevated position. The honor and responsibility of being an Executive Secretary are rarely given to the spring chick (unless she substitutes efficiency with a lower-cut blouse). The typical Executive Secretary looks prim, is fiercely loyal, types memos, and blocks phone calls. In a more value-added role, she occupies a central position in the manufacture, manipulation, and distribution of executive opinion, of so-called knowledge based on her belief that the higher echelons in a corporation have a greater claim to own the truth.

Although she works close to the source where official company information is produced, her biggest claim is not that she knows EVERYTHING (for this, see the Janitor); but she THINKS she knows what's IMPORTANT. And about what is important she has definite opinions.

Her opinions are strongly colored by convictions held by the executive she is chartered to serve and protect. No wonder: Her noblest assignment and the true test of her value are to leak his preferences to the non-executive folks beneath. In some cases she may be asked to lie *with* him (as the beautiful, young, and warm girl Abishag did with another old and cold executive, King David of the Bible, reported in 1 Kings 1:3,4). In corporate cultures with a more highly developed morality, such as Fortune 1000 companies, she is only required to lie *for* him. For instance, when a customer calls with a complaint while the executive is picking his nose in the sanctum of his wood-paneled office, she will say, "He is in a meeting. I can't bug him now."

On occasion, she will fall in love with her executive, a love that is never reciprocated unless sex can serve temporarily as a synonym for the L-word and only when the air is completely clean and the wood-paneled office is completely soundproof. Possible complications (because the air isn't quite clean or the office not completely soundproof) are resolved at her expense. In such cases, her association with the company may be dissolved, while his sins are more easily exculpated by tradition (these things happen, they always have) and psychological excuses (the stress, the long hours). Executives have a certain moral expense account that they may use with impunity.

While subject to these risks and temptations in the antechamber to executive power, the Executive Secretary exerts a considerable influence on visitors. When she overhears Mr. Somebody criticizing her boss she will defend her executive first and tell on Mr. Somebody later. The talented corporate careerist, such as the Fair-Haired Boy and the Survivor, must be on excellent footing with the Executive Secretary. Being polite and generally subservient is not enough. Flowers, compliments, and a genteel flirt will be appreciated. Even more brownie points may be gathered when these non-executives share with the Executive Secretary the gossip they've heard in the bowels of the corporation, with the understanding that she in turn will funnel this tittle-tattle, together with her color commentary, to her boss.

On the Wednesday of the last full week in April, the corporate world has for more than fifty years celebrated Secretary's Day, now officially and euphoniously called Administrative Professional's Day, so that admin assistants, receptionists, mail room clerks, and other administrative professionals can be honored as well, leaving 364 days where they are largely forgotten. The Executive Secretary, who never changed her name to Executive Administrative Professional, will be invited to lunch with her Executive, who'll order crème brûlée for dessert and say that he "really appreciates the hard work" she has put in all year. She is offered the afternoon off, but prefers to go back to work, that is, to be driven back to work in the executive's company car, for all administrative professionals to see. On the way back to her chamber in the executive suite her body language lets everybody know: I may not rule, but I reign.

The Janitor

In a modern corporation, skill and knowledge are distributed over many different experts, but infinite awareness, coupled with surprising insight and broad understanding at a much more holistic level, is concentrated in only one individual: the Janitor.

The characterization of the Janitor as a doorkeeper places him in the same league as the other two great porters in mythical history: canny old Saint Peter, concierge at the Pearly Gates of Heaven, and his canine counterpart, the three-headed dog Cerberus, who is guarding the entrance to Hades, the underground abode of sinners and Non-Christians.

The Janitor is not powerful *ex officio*, but like Saint Peter he knows people and their affairs. He is kind, until you draw his wrath, for instance by pulling rank or being uncivil. Like Cerberus, he doesn't use many words, but his few words have bite. He appears plain and simple only to the superficial mind that has forgotten that his namesake is Janus, the god who is identified with gates swinging either way (think saloon doors in movies of the Old West), signifying the beginning and the end of all mortal things, the past and the future, the simultaneity of opposites. Because of his gift to represent opposites, it is dangerous and self-defeating to take the Janitor simply at face value. He knows the haves and the have-nots, converses with the CEO and the cleaning crew, understands what mergers are and what a plumber does.

Many of his daily tasks are mundane. He locks away the extra light bulbs and the spare rolls of toilet paper. He opens up in the morning and closes down at night. Being everywhere and nowhere in particular, he isn't anywhere out of place. This is how he knows who is talking to whom, and when, and why. He can tell who is hot and who is not. He knows the Fair-Haired Boys and the Has-beens, the Survivors and Hands-Ons and every secretary. Since he's the first to hear baseball scores and stock prices (thanks to the old cell phone in his overall pockets) everybody listens to him, and since he is an even better listener, with eyes that seem to reflect a deep interest in what is being said, everybody likes to talk to him. People with more problems than power (technicians, accountants, middle managers) prefer to confide in him rather than in their bosses. People with power (vice presidents, the CEO) tell him more than they'd ever tell their spouses or mistresses.

Especially heartfelt and symbiotic is his relationship with the Executive Secretary. He does small favors for her, moves her desk, fixes a sliding door with a penny stuck in it, and repairs her heater in winter. She reciprocates by letting him know little tidbits of executive banter overheard between her boss, the VP, and the CEO, and she knows that these bits of information will eventually make it into the corporation at large. In return, the Janitor relays a recent rumor to her, explains why several middle managers are miffed at "her" VP, and he'll speak up for the modest request of ordinary employees (ergonomic chairs, better window coverings, a cleaner lunch room), hoping, not without good reason and successful precedent, that the Executive Secretary will find a way to let her VP know.

One day the Janitor watched on TV another Janitor, the character played by Neil Flynn in the series "Scrubs". At first he was irritated, but then he shrugged and said, "This Janitor has no class."

The Know-It-All

The Know-It-All is a real-life example of the fictitious character Clifford C. Clavin, Jr., who played a postal worker in the television show *Cheers* and described himself as the "winged nut that holds western civilization together."

The species of the Know-It-All can be found in all walks of corporate life.

There is, for example, the subspecies of the precocious and book-smart MBA graduate. When he polished a big red apple in his thesis by pretending to take his professor's post-modern economic theories seriously, his professor predicted a bright future for him and wrote glowing recommendations to bolster his meager resume. This is the first step on the way to becoming a schmuck. And a schmuck, once hired, turns quickly into a Know-It-All.

As a consequence of such academic endorsement, the young MBA sets out to change the world at large and "his" company in particular. After his bookish knowledge has proved irrelevant by a year's worth of hands-on experience in the corporate world, his conceit of knowing more gives way to "knowing better," and that being right is inferior to being righteous. Add a pinch of smugness, and a Know-It-All is born.

In addition to this whippersnapper Know-It-All, there is also the old miser Know-It-All, a veteran corporate war horse. He never made it high up the ranks, but he knows it all because he (thinks he) has seen it all: "Been there, done that." Compared to the buzz of change promoted by the young MBA, he is the advocate of the status quo. In the court of company meetings he counters every new proposal with, "I can't encourage this, I won't endorse that, I've seen it all before. It doesn't work. Trust me."

Related to the miser Know-It-All is the veteran middle manager, who knew the company founder. This privilege has built up an ego that will simply not tolerate dissent. He is a Know-It-All *ex officio*, in his own estimation. He cannot imagine being wrong. Hence he must be right. His logic is as tight as his vest. He is closed to further debates because, after all, his time served in the company speaks louder in his favor than the modish clamor of parvenus, no matter how good their resumes may be.

A third sub-species, a more intellectual Know-It-All, appears in Vladimir Nabokov's novel *The Gift*. "He was self-satisfied, discursive, obtuse, and germanically ignorant; i.e., he treated everything he did not know with skepticism."

On an even more academic note, I must mention Leo Buscaglia, the late USC faculty member who was known as "the professor of love." His aphorism, "Those who think they know it all have no way of finding out they don't" is part of a larger picture where the serious affliction of anosognosia rules (see below), and where Donald Rumsfeld has made his mark. Here is how:

First, take someone who knows her stuff, say an experienced software engineer named Kate. She will likely consider herself a specialist and not claim to know it all. Kate's professional knowledge is limited – she may be an authority in the computer language Perl; and within the realm of Perl she knows what she knows.

Second, going a step further, there is lovely Muriel. She also has her area of know-how and know-what, which, let's say, is cloud computing. Being a researcher and endowed with a skeptic mind, she is highly aware of what she doesn't know – "know not yet," she adds, because she may yet learn the as-yet-unknown by googling, asking around, or looking at a textbook. Her friend Thaddeus, an unemployed philosopher, insists, however, that there are certain "things" between heaven and earth, in poetry, music, mathematics, even in cloud computing, that will forever be beyond us humans with our nimble hands and monkey brains. Socrates, says Thaddeus, elevated the "know what you don't know" to the philosophical principle "know that you won't ever know," and with this

Socrates had defined what Thaddeus calls "a modest, resigned wisdom."

Where do the Know-It-All and his self-deception come in? Through a door that former Secretary of State Donald Rumsfeld opened when he coined his famous phrase of the "unknown unknowns." At the time, he received a lot of guff for this expression, because it was seen as another example of his well-known verbal obfuscation that had served him well in clouding the truth about "weapons of mass destruction" and the "war on terrorism." On second thought, however, and in a curiously roundabout way, Rumsfeld was onto something that has been called Anosognosia: *not knowing what you don't know*. The term Anosognosia [from a=without, nosos=disease, gnosis=knowledge] was originally, by its creator Joseph Babinski, applied to people who had suffered a stroke, were paralyzed on one side, and appeared not to know, or not to acknowledge, this. They acted as if they were healthy. But since then, it has been recognized more broadly as a cognitive affliction called the Dunning-Kruger Effect and is applied especially to people who are so incompetent that they don't know how incompetent they really are. Not knowing *what* they don't know, and not knowing *that* they don't know *what* they don't know, they are the opposites of Socrates' wise men. They are fools. But since their Anosognosia prevents them from being aware of their foolishness, they assume that their ignorance about the unknown is the same as knowing all. Ergo, they are exactly the Know-It-Alls who are the winged nuts of corporations.

The Staff Member

Only a mediocre person is always at his best.

In a corporation, employees without a particular title or rank are called staff members. They are the foot soldiers, infantry men, the peasants, or, in the language of chess, the pawns. While a pawn may attain a special value in certain situation on the chessboard, his movements are severely restricted and he is generally considered the weakest piece among all chess figures. In a corporation, the staff member's weakness shows in multiple ways. He is not only replaceable and an "at will" employee (he can be let go with or without cause at any time) – most lower echelon employees share this uncertainty; he also must rely solely on his skills, because he has no reports and therefore no political power, which is also called "clout." His corporate welfare depends on one man or woman: his direct manager.

Nevertheless, the staff member shares with the chess pawn other, more positive features, even strengths. He shows up in higher numbers and can, when he is clever, form alliances and in this way, like pawns in a chess game, obtain a strategic position without individual clout. In this position, a pawn is often defensive, part of a bulwark protecting the king or other more valuable pieces. Likewise, staff members may lend strength and protection to others they value or need, such as IT managers, personnel managers, embattled department heads, and others. Just as a pawn always threatens to capture a piece of the opposing party by approaching it obliquely from the left or right, so a staff member can do harm, in many indirect and underhanded ways, to competing or otherwise unwelcome employees. If a staff member is very skillful, he may, like the pawn who's successful at "queening", catapult himself and his team's game to a higher level of importance.

However, most staff members don't reach a high level by their skill alone. They have to use other means to advance. Take, for instance, him who can't think or code but dresses well. This type of staff member cannot exist without a tie. His matching shirts are freshly pressed and starched armor-like, subdued in color and design. Engineers call him a "stuffed shirt" or an "artificial man". He is known as a "Man, But Artificial", an MBA. He is the purest type of the Corporate Spirit. We have already encountered the Corporate Gentleman as an example of this type. The Spirit oozes out of his suit into the environment. Advertising the Spirit justifies his existence in the company. Without him, there would not be a Corporate Spirit.

Following Plato, who calls a man wise who imitates the one and only God, the Corporate Staff Member acts like the paperback copy of the CEO, the one and only God whom he often sees and always greets.

Loyalty is his key word. This does not mean that he will die for the company, but that he will live off it as long as possible.

Speaking about his work involves the use of many words like "we" and "us" and "our". Not that his work can be described precisely. In general terms, however, his work has to do with something called 'support'. He is a singer in the Big Chorus just as the always-smarter alecks in Greek tragedies were. He constitutes the audience on stage, the background "in the know", and the hired claqueur of "our" achievements.

When the company has drifted into difficulties, he is the one who knows all the good reasons, economical, political, personal; and the better excuses, economical, political, personal. He also offers cautious remedies to his peers and distributes mild blames towards management, in whispered words that are in accord with the Corporate Spirit and the CEO, whom he greets even more devotedly in harder times.

To outsiders his optimism is a riddle. They wonder about his facial expression, confident, devout, and mild like a parson's smile. His children go to parochial schools, and at parent meetings he

talks eagerly to another parent at the school, the Corporate Gentleman, about values and the Corporate Spirit. He is well informed.
He is always at his best.

The Loquacious

(After Theophrastus)

Loquacity means incontinence of the tongue, or diarrhea of words. Whatever you may be talking about, he interrupts you by saying, "You don't know a thing, I know the whole story, and if you listen to me you'll learn what's really going on." If you continue on the subject, he will interject again: "Thanks for reminding me, how helpful a conversation is! You are right, what you just said, I had almost forgotten. You've taken the words out of my mouth. I was just waiting to see if you think about it as I do."

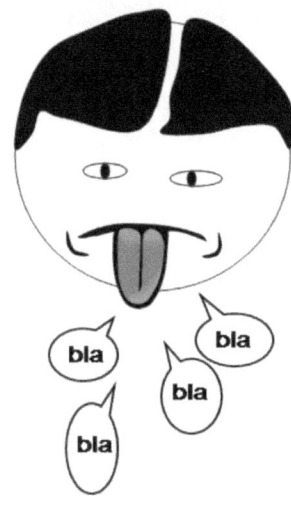

In this way he seizes upon every opportunity to talk. Everybody with whom he converses is afraid of taking a breath lest he'll take over immediately. Having gotten on the nerves of everybody, he will turn up where groups gather, discussing some kind of business, and he practically puts them to flight with his constant prattle. For instance, he enters training sessions and interrupts the lessons by chatting with their teachers. If anyone leaves in order to avoid the Loquacious, he follows him to his home.

He is informed of what's going on in meetings, and he makes it his business to tell everybody about it, wherever he goes. Once he has an audience, he goes further and describes at great length what happened with, say, the takeover of Compaq by HP, which, he'll tell you, occurred under the reign of Dame Carly, and from there he talks about Oracle's purchase of Sun, and of course he never forgets the role he played in certain staff meetings and exactly what he said then. He never notices when people get sick of his bragging, or when he bores them utterly, or when they simply want to leave.

A Loquacious puts a stop to business and pleasure alike. At work he distracts his colleagues, at the theater he prevents those sitting near him from enjoying the play, and at dinner parties his chatter prevents his neighbor at the table from eating.

He will openly confess that it is difficult for a talker like him to hold his tongue. "The tongue," he'd says, "is like a loose bell hanging in a tower, it must be moved and rung." He admits that he'd rather appear as noisy as a flight of swallows than be silent like a mouse. He will bear it gladly when people laugh at his folly, even his children, who, when they want to go to sleep, will say to him: "Come on, Daddy, tell us a tale so that we may fall asleep."

[Note: This corporate character "The Loquacious", was (freely) translated from Theophrastus' seventh character Peri Lalias. Some phrases were taken from Francis Howell's translation, published by Josiah Taylor, Architectural Library, London, 1824. I prefer this old and slightly odd edition to Isaac Taylor's (1836) translation and to the pleasant but anachronistic rendering by Charles E. Bennett and William A. Hammond, London (1902). The definite edition of the Greek text was published in 1897 by the Leipziger Philologische Gesellschaft.]

The Yes-Man

Contrary to what Henry David Thoreau's says in his essay "On the Duty of Civil Disobedience," the Yes-Man thinks that we should be subjects first, and men afterwards. The Yes-Man takes "subject" literally, as in sub-jected to the demands of the law, the country, and his corporation. For Thoreau, man and woman (collectively "men") are free and conscientious beings, who write the law, make up the country, form a corporation, and should therefore be their masters. O no, answers the Yes-Man, being conscientious is second and subordinated to saying Yes and to paying allegiance to the collective whole, and in particular to the collected rules and regulations of a corporation.

Translating Thoreau's term "citizen" in his essay as "employee of a corporation" and his "legislator" as "manager," we may ask: "Must the employee in a corporation ever for a moment, or in the least degree, resign his conscience to his manager?" For a Yes-Man the answer is clear: "Yes, not only for a moment, but forever!" And when Thoreau asks rhetorically, "Why has every man a conscience, then?" and adding to this, "It is truly enough said, that a corporation has no conscience," the Yes-Man, as a matter of habit, may again simply nod or repeat what he's heard from his managers, "A conscience tends to reduce productivity."

"But," Thoreau would respond, citing his own words, "a corporation of conscientious men is a corporation with a conscience." The Yes-Man railroads such a subtle (albeit legally and logically fragile) assertion by borrowing a malicious wise-crack from Sam Slick: "Going through life with a conscience is like driving your car with the brakes on."

The problem here is as well-known as it is complex. For man to be conscientious in Thoreau's understanding, he does not follow the obligations of rules because they are rules, but he will only do "at any time what I think right." And in order to create a collective corporate conscience, he must expend a special kind of moral energy. This special energy resides in the backbone of somebody who has preserved an ounce of independence and a grain of self-respect. This ounce and this grain are hard to obtain, and even harder to maintain, once the "values" of the Corporate Spirit have replaced the native marrow in the backbone of a corporate citizen.

With such spiritual marrow in his bones and an ever-ready "Yes" on his lips, the Yes-Man is equipped to get ahead in his company, at least up to a comfortable middle-manager position. In meetings, he listens very carefully to managers to whom he has resigned his conscience, and approves their opinions with periodic nods "Very true, yes, very true."

The Yes-Man has a favorite book, and yes, it is called *Yes Man*, written by Danny Wallace who, for an entire year, chose to say "Yes" to any offer that came his way, including Internet solicitations and credit card offers, and to say "Yes" to any opinions of his managers. This entertaining book was adapted into a so-so movie with goofy Jim Carrey. The corporate Yes-Man has seen it twenty times and owns the DVD, which he plays when he has guests.

It is a fact that some Yes-Men say "Yes" their entire life, because they see their best chance of survival in staying in the good graces of the strongest – the boss, the wealthy, the powerful. With a "Hurray" on their lips they would follow the dashing lieutenant who's leading the charge in war. However, for other Yes-Men, the sugary diet of Yes, without the salty taste of No will lead to a fatal bending of the backbone into a permanent kowtow, leaving the Yes-Man in a crooked state of a groveling servant, a moral hunchpback, capable only of bowing and scraping.

Slowly, inevitably, the Yes-Man will become a No-Body.

Note: Do not confuse the Corporate Yes-Man with "The Yes Men" by Andy Bichlbaum and Mike Bonanno, see http://en.wikipedia.org/wiki/The_Yes_Men. These ironically named Yes-

Men play elaborate spoofs on the mighty, the wealthy, the selfish – men and corporations.

The Quality Manager

The Quality Manager is responsible for "the very idea of Quality", but not for the quality of any particular product. The reason for this rather philosophical definition of his role is the unwritten "constitution" of a mature, enlightened corporation which states that the three branches: Product, Sales, and Quality must be separate and independent. "Product" includes Research and Development, "Sales" relies on Marketing and Advertising, and "Quality" is the keeper of Rules. In this sense, the three corporate divisions mirror the well-known separation of the Legislative, the Executive, and the Judiciary powers. From this higher standpoint it is understandable that the role of the Quality Manager is abstract and bookish, just like the role of justices and judges. From this model it is also clear that (as the Quality Manager repeatedly emphasizes), "Quality does not *write* the Rules, Quality does not *make* the Product. Quality is the *referee* and *champion* of the idea of Quality *per se*, ideally without ever laying hands on the product itself."

To exemplify this hands-off attitude, the Corporate Quality Manager will step in to assert, for instance, that Quality, capitalized, cannot be *inspected into* a product just as good manners cannot be *spanked into* a schoolboy. In the same way, he continues, that a product cannot be *punished* for being bad. Instead, R&D needs to *design* quality into the product according to strict standards, just as parents need to *raise* their children according to strict standards.

The distance between Quality *per se* (the very idea) and quality *per diem* (the actual product) requires of the Quality Manager as much philosophical detachment as it demands his messianic involvement. Keeping this distinction in mind is not a contradiction for him. He has a Sony TV set at home but displays a sign in his office imploring everyone in red and blue capital letters, BUY AMERICAN!

The Quality Manager is aware of the different roles that the Japanese and *our* US quality cultures have played since *we* won the great Pacific War. "For instance," he says, "the Japanese improved their quality first and created the Deming Prize afterwards as an outward sign of *achievement* and continual reminder to keep improving their products. We in the US have short-circuited some of this rather slow and laborious evolution and created the Baldrige Award to revolutionize quality *advertising*."

There are already many signs that this strategy has worked for us Americans. For instance, over the past years it has become easier to return merchandise to stores hassle-free – as soon as the buyer senses a discrepancy between the advertisement and his own expectation. In the official American quality literature (see: Forbes, Fortune, Business Week, Quality Progress) this is called the "Nordstrom Effect."

Currently, as the Quality Manager points out, there are "efforts underway, supported by the Federal Government and the Trump Empire, to proclaim another month as Quality Month, so that we have two and the Japanese still only have none. Negotiations with January and July are making good progress."

The Angel Investor

In professional sports, in football, baseball, basketball, and soccer, retired players sometimes become coaches. Based on their reputation, they advertise that they'll repeat their individual success in a new role as strategists and team motivators from the sidelines. Mike Ditka played for the Chicago Bears, was their Rookie of the Year, won the Super Bowl with the Dallas Cowboys, with whom he again won the Super Bowl as their Assistant Coach. Then he became head coach of the Bears and won with them Superbowl XX. Other examples are Dusty Baker in Baseball and Steve Kerr in Basketball. The metamorphosis from being famous as a player to making a team win trophies does not always work. Jürgen Klinsmann was a great soccer player, but as a coach without fortune. If the transition works, the coach is a genius. If it doesn't, the team is blamed and sent packing. The coach is fired but keeps his salary. After another season, he hires on with a new club – until his reputation, which is his capital, recovers or is depleted and gone.

An Angel Investor follows a similar path. He succeeds in a company and makes stacks of money. He could now feather his nest and enjoy life. But that is not enough. He feels that there is something special, almost divine about him. He has grown wings. His ego soars and so does his belief that he can reverse the process for even bigger paybacks: use some money from the stack, buy (part of) a company, and repeat the individual success at a large scale. More often than not, the gamble doesn't work. Employees are blamed and laid off. The Angel Investor loses some feathers. If, however, he succeeds, he graduates from Angel to Semi-God.

Since becoming a Semi-God is not a sure thing, Angels have been known to pool the risk and band together in larger flocks. These investor nests exist close to large industry parks, for instance on Sand Hill Road, in the Silicon Valley, California. Here, in sleek offices, "the next big things" are hatched by Semi-Gods in expensive suits. Whom to fund and when and with how much – that is shrouded in secrecy. But often it happens like this: Entrepreneurs strut their stuff like fashion models on a runway. One after another, they present their collection, their ideas cast in Powerpoint, sometimes with a prototype "proving" the concept. A very small percentage of these ideas are funded, and when one of them takes off, like Google or Facebook, one or more of the Angels-turned-Semigods take credit first and their immense reward soon afterwards.

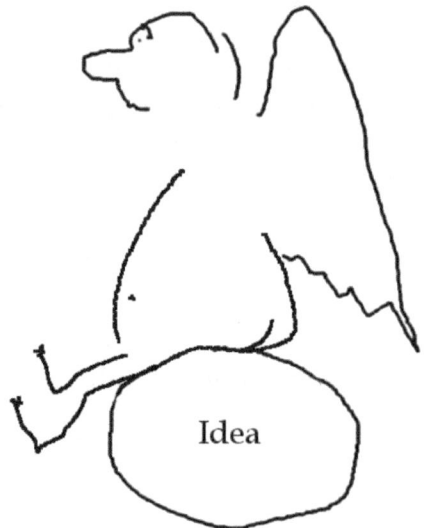

Once part of an investor nest, an Angel is called a Venture Capitalist. It is essential to understand both terms, VENTURE and CAPITAL.

VENTURE: The verb "to venture" is quite descriptive, embracing the combined connotations of risk, hazard, gamble and adventure. It suggests the temptation of being exposed to possible loss or damage, but is fueled by the hope of gaining financial advantage. It plays to a gambler's willingness to speculate and lay bets, and to the thrill of winning.

CAPITAL: One of the non-standard (post Marx) definitions of responsible (sic!) capitalism most congenial to the spirit of Corporate America was implied by Malcolm Forbes's bi-weekly paternal advice: "With all thy getting get understanding." Trying not to be side-tracked by the archaic "thy", the reader senses that the emphasis is clearly on the verb "get." The first "getting" in Forbes' short sentence requires, but lacks a direct object. It is easy enough to supply: getting the biggest piece of the pie at the lowest price, and without tax implications - that is what capitalism à la Forbes is all about.

It's also about slaughtering and misunderstanding a biblical quote. Forbes' quote "With all thy getting get understanding" perverts the actual meaning of the biblical Proverb 4:7, which is really about wisdom, not about "thy getting" more money or power or influence: "Wisdom is the principal thing; therefore get wisdom; and with all thy getting get understanding" (King James Version).

Putting aside Forbes' trivial biz-mag advise and listening instead to Professor Joseph A. Schumpeter, the Venture Capitalist is the modern juxtaposition of capitalist and entrepreneur. Schumpeter knew that it takes more than an invention to make a profit. He built a new theory around the linchpin "innovation", whose two components "capital" and "enterprise" are combined in the Angel Investor's simple philosophy: "Have money, will invest in company."

The Salesperson

All humans, says Aristotle in the opening sentence of his book on Metaphysics, have the innate urge to pursue learning and knowledge. This is a statement made without much empirical evidence. More recent observations in Corporate America have corrected Aristotle's view of what is truly the essence of human nature. All humans, this new research has shown, have the innate urge to Buy and to Sell (in short: BS).

Using a classical syllogism, and using the fact that absolutely no human frailty is alien to us, we can easily see why we in America are world champions in BS:

If all humans love BS, and

if we Americans are absolutely human,

then we must absolutely love BS.

Many generations ago, our very own philosopher, Henry David Thoreau of Walden Pond, taught us in his essay "The Bean Field" to pay more attention to the S than to the B: *patrem familias vendacem, non emacem esse oportet*: "It befits the head of every household to more eagerly sell than to frantically buy." In other words, for Thoreau the BS ought to be unbalanced in favor of the export over the import, lest a trade deficit will result. In recent times, such a deficit has indeed been observed, due to disobeying Thoreau and increasing the import of oil from the Middle East and buying goods from China. Andy Warhol, a sage who was more up-to-date and in tune with our modern psyche than Thoreau, stated: "Buying is much more American than thinking." Instead of "thinking," he could have said "selling." Or perhaps "thinking" and "selling" are synonymous for true Americans?

Thoreau advises us to sell and Warhol responds with America's penchant for buying. It should also be noted – in order to give "thinking" its due – that another one of Aristotle's deeper insights, that true wisdom shows in the ability to think in first principles and act on them pragmatically, does underlie our economic transactions as an axiom to this day. Indeed, our desire to BS is founded on the economic axiom of supply and demand. To go a step further, however, economists today have creatively combined the ideas of Thoreau, Warhol, and Aristotle. They are telling us:

1) Buy low and sell high; this is mainly for individual gain and applies to stocks and real estate. 2) Buy American; this kind of "buying" is often called "shopping," and we do this for ourselves, for entertainment, but also as a patriotic duty, regardless of price and quality. 3) Always think that the principle of supply and demand can be influenced by pragmatic tinkering and tampering with a customer's soul through advertisements and thus creating a demand that wasn't there before.

The wisdom assembled above is embodied in *homo venditor*, the salesperson. There are two extreme cases of this species. One is described by Earl Shorris in his book *A Nation of Salesmen: The Tyranny of the Market and the Subversion of Culture*. Shorris depicts the salesperson as both dangerous and afflicted. He or she creates a reality through the "mix of mind and matter that is perception" and, as mediator between desire and information, spawns new desires we didn't know we had. On this borderline between morality and shamelessness you'll also find the gimcrack salesperson as actor whose motivation is not even siring needs or making money, but "just the sell, the getting-over, in itself."

Usually there is an emotional ceremonial of transaction going on between salesperson and customer, an unholy ritual during which not only money and merchandise change hands, but also several cloying compliments before and after BS. Vladimir Nabokov, in his otherwise unrelated book *The Gift*, mentions "those lowered lashes of modest price ... the nobility of the discount ... the altruism of advertisements." One of his characters, a certain Alexandra Yakovlevna, confessed that during shopping "she is morally transplanted to a special world where she grows intoxicated from the wine of honesty, from the sweetness of mutual favors, and replies to the salesman's incarnadine smile with a smile of radiant rapture."

The smile, though probably less open-mouth and pink-palate colored than in Nabokov's salesman, is a paradigm for the other extreme specimen of the *homo venditor*, Arthur Miller's salesman Willy Loman. "Willy Loman," writes Miller about him, "never made a lot of money. His name was never in the paper. He's not the finest character that ever lived. But he's a human being ... He's a man way out there in the blue, riding on a smile and a shoeshine." Loman was not the flashy MBA sporting a yellow tie with black polka dots. He was the American Everyman with spots on his hat and rumpled trousers. But like all salespersons, like all Americans, he's "got to dream. It comes with the territory."

The Wannabe

Every night, the Wannabe hums his favorite song, the Spice Girls' pop single "Wannabe," where the refrain goes like this:

> I'll tell you what I want, what I really really want,
> So tell me what you want, what you really really want,
> I wanna, I wanna, I wanna, I wanna, I wanna really
> really really wanna zigazig ha.

The Has-Been thinks fondly of the past wishing it were the present, whereas the Wannabe thinks fondly of himself in the present, imagining it to be the future. The Wannabe spells "not yet" n-o-w, the Has-been spells "future" n-e-v-e-r. They seem to be living on opposite planets, and should they ever meet at the water cooler and shake hands, they might annihilate each other like matter and antimatter. Beneath the Wannabe's wide-eyed graduation photo the yearbook editors wrote the prophetic caption "Most likely to pretend to succeed," and a smarty-pants had edited this label and written over it "Most likely to succeed to pretend."

When he started working as a marketing associate, his business card read already "Marketing Specialist", which he then changed to "Senior Marketing Specialist," while telling customers that he acts "in lieu" of the Marketing Director and works "very closely" with the VP of Marketing. Such a stretch of the literal truth on business cards and on resumes has been cited as cause for dismissal, but in this case a savvy Wannabe could claim bragging as his fundamental right, a right not explicitly listed in the US Constitution, but protected by the Ninth Amendment in the Bill of Rights, where it says: "The enumeration in the Constitution, of certain rights, shall not be construed to deny or disparage others retained by the people." The Wannabe can reasonably refer to Harvard historian Bernard Bailyn, who in a speech at the White House on the subject of the Ninth Amendment said that the Ninth Amendment refers to "a universe of rights, possessed by the people – latent rights, still to be evoked and enacted into law ... a reservoir of other, unenumer- ated rights that the people retain, which in time may be enacted into law." So far, however, a Wannabe's "bragging right" joins other non-explicit residuum rights such as the right to privacy and a woman's right to an abortion as "not unqualified or unfettered." (Roe v. Wade, 314 F. Supp. 1217 at 1223 (1970))

To be fair, I will mention that others, including the late Supreme Court Justice Antonin Scalia, agreed with Professor Laurence Tribe's uninspired view against bragging rights: "It is a common error, but an error nonetheless, to talk of 'ninth amendment rights.' The ninth amendment is not a source of rights as such; it is simply a rule about how to read the Constitution." But this opinion is self-defeating, as a smart Lawyer-Wannabe told me, because bragging is "free speech" and protected by the First Amendment. When a Wannabe resorts to lies as his "weapons and arms" in corporate competitions for raises and positions, the Second Amendment protects him by guaranteeing that such a "right of the people to keep and bear Arms, shall not be infringed."

The Wannabe competes with his spiritual brother, the Empty-Suit. They are both actors on the corporate stage, but they have chosen different roles for themselves. The Empty-Suit is the sleek prop speaking hollow words, a paper tiger without teeth, a grinning mask with no face behind it. The Wannabe chooses his own mask, but not to hide, but to advertise himself as the character suggested by his mask. Sometimes he is the fanatic jester advising the king the way Andy Garcia's character eggs on Godfather Al Pacino in Godfather III. Sometimes he is the pretender to a throne, like Jack Cade (gang leader in Shakespeare's Henry VI, Part 2) who lauds himself "Valiant I am ... I am able to endure much ... I fear neither sword nor fire ... "

Keep being a pretender, Wannabe, behind an assumed mask that substitutes for your real being, Wannabe, but the time will come when you have to answer the Spice Girls' urgent call, "Tell me who do you (really!) think you are?"

> I said who do you think you are
> Oh, oh (do you think you are, I said)
> Ooh some kind of superstar (oh, oh, oh)
> You have got to swing it, shake it, move it, make it
> Who do you think you are
> Trust it, use it, prove it, groove it
> Show me how good you are
> Swing it, shake it, move it, make it
> Who do you think you are
> Trust it, use it, prove it, groove it
> Show how good you are

The Visionary

He is the Executive Seer, the Corporate Prophet. He is like the holy man Kalchas in Homer's Iliad, who was by far the best of the bird interpreters and who knew all things, the things past and the things future.

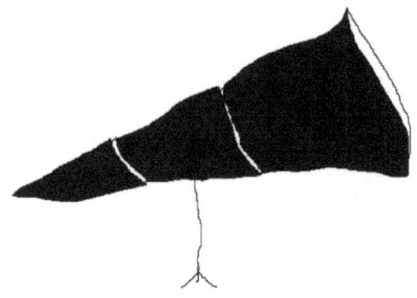

His mind's far-sighted eye envisions a telescopic picture of the future, but it is the power of his words that will rally the crowd around what he sees and what needs to be done. As a literary trope, the ability of matching fitting words to a picture and thus verbally recreating an image beyond a mere description is called Ekphrasis, "word-imaging." The received wisdom "A picture is worth a thousand words" applies only when words are cheap or put together in pedestrian ways. In sharper minds, where the imagination is keenly alive, a thousand words can evoke a million pictures and wake up a billion neurons, and moreover, converge into a single call for action. Therefore, the verbal imaging of a Visionary is more than the rhetorical flip side to an illustration that assigns pictorial equivalents to passages of speech. It shapes the corporate future.

Ideally, he has a voice that trembles between the trusted bass of Walter Cronkite and the soulful baritone of Billy Graham. Being a master of the "not yet," he does not have to prove his point here and now as a salesperson or engineer must. His art lies in articulating and making visible the invisible while it still remains unseen.

When he speaks, Merlin's smile plays around his lips, and through the mild glaze of his eyes he looks a bit like the blind seer Tiresias. Already in the underworld after an eventful life (seven years of which he spent as a woman!), Tiresias was still able to look ahead and tell the visiting Odysseus about the rest of his journey and his troublesome homecoming. As is usual with predictions by others, Odysseus didn't obey one of Tiresias' warnings (not to slaughter and eat cattle on Sicily), but at least he was more circumspect when approaching his homestead where, as Tiresias had predicted, a swarm of idle noblemen was trying to seduce his wife Penelope. That is typical: people seek out visionaries and listen to them, but follow only parts of their advice.

The Visionary will explain that his deliverable, the articulation of a possible future, is not just a "vision thing," nor is it a craft of eschatology. Predictions about the return to paradise or the coming of Armageddon are not his métier. His time horizon is shorter, five or ten years at most (which Wall Street wants shortened to three months), and the gratification of being right is awarded him in hindsight only.

With massive fame and fortune awaiting the successful Visionary, the run-of-the-mill employee like you and me may ask: How do I become a Visionary? There is no reason why you shouldn't. The following rules will get you there in five easy steps.

1. *Predict orders of magnitude improvement.* In 1977, the first Apple II computer ran at 1 MHz speed. A clever Visionary would "see" the possibility of 10 MHz processors and describe the benefits of such blazing speed. In 1986, the Apple IIGS reached 10 MHz, then 16 MHz, using so-called accelerators. Similarly, the original puny 4 KB of RAM increased 10-fold and much, much more – giving the Visionary fodder for his *order-of-magnitude* visions almost yearly.

2. *Minimize or maximize*: Speaking of memory, miniaturization has proven a fertile ground for predictable predictions over

the years: 8 inch, 5.25 inch, and 3.5 inch floppy disks have long given way to flash drives so small they can be worn as ear rings, while the capacity has dramatically increased. The visionary principle of *much more and much smaller* is a trick that the late Steve Jobs, chief Visionary at Apple, had perfected. In other words, go for the extreme, as long as these are not zero and not infinity.

3. *Extrapolate*: This visionary technique may also be called *integrate and follow the trend*. John Bogle did just that when he invented the first retail index fund, combining the buying power of many small investors with the benefit of mixing securities (thus diversifying) that follow, by and large, a standard success measure (an index like the S&P 500). A further advantage was that in 1975 the IRS allowed IRAs, which became the ideal framework for Bogle's invention, now known as Vanguard 500 Index Fund. Other examples of integrating fashionable features are the iPhone, Blackberry, and later the iPad.

4. *Playing opposites*: When the Visionary wants people to think that he came up with something truly original and out-of-the-box, he will take something old and known, and proposed the opposite. He would recommend dividing up an inert hierarchical company into several more agile independent business units, and five years later he'd urge that wastefully independent divisions ought to be consolidated behind a unified strategy. He may suggest outsourcing customer support for cost reasons, and two years later advise that in-sourcing customer service will increase tax benefits.

5. *Apply the Hawthorne effect*: Visionaries rarely focus on you and me, but when employee productivity, or lack thereof, is discussed, he will quickly come up with ways to implement the Hawthorne effect, according to which productivity in-

creases simply by the fact that the Visionary is studying the issue and managers are paying attention.

The Visionary must sometimes act in the role of Corporate Evangelist. Davy Crocket once said, "I can outspeak any man." But the Visionary-cum-Evangelist is not just any man. He is the carrier of good news in the guise of hyperbole, the silver-tongued master of tall-talk, as the pioneers called it. He never goes out shooting without the long bow.

As a modern seer and pioneer, he is the corporate avant-garde of propaganda. He is a brother-in-spirit to the ring-tailed roarer and stump-speaker, whose tall talk is highfalutin and flamboyant ballyhoo worthy of Sam Slick's credo "Braggin' saves advertisin'."

And so the Visionary-Evangelist has become the latter-day version of the Yankee peddler, a huckster and hawker who, in Paul Bunyan's Natural History was called a Teakettler because the noise he makes resembles that of a boiling teakettle. Clouds of vapor issue from his mouth and condense on his ever-growing Pinocchio nose.

The Customer

The well-known scene in the Garden of Eden, where Eve is se-
duced to eat fruit from the forbidden tree, is usually interpreted as
mankind's fall from grace. It should be viewed as a brilliant sales
job by the snake. Eve was the first gullible Customer in a long line
to come, and Adam the first man to foot the bill. The snake got the
bad reputation that salespeople still have to live with; but its excuse shows a rationale that is as valid now as it was then: "The
Customer wanted it, and she is always right."

Since those early days, Corporate America has been motivated
by what the Customer wants, not what she needs. Of course, corporations have rarely given her exactly what she wants either; but
luckily for the economy, the Customer often doesn't know exactly
what she wants. Hence she asks for everything, and, when lured by
coupons, frequent flier miles, or tax breaks, will usually buy something. "Save more by spending more," is a counter-intuitive, yet
wonderfully successful sales pitch. Realizing that a Customer must
be told what she wants, Corporate America has enlisted Advertising. This industry publishes its self-fulfilling prophecies under the
motto that choice is freedom, and, by implication, that buying is
patriotic. Against this, a Customer has no defense, or in football
terms: Corporate America and Advertising are matched against
customers like a professional team quarterbacked by the referee
playing against a gaggle of grade school amateurs.

Corporate America can therefore address its Customers after the
image that Advertising and her prettier sister, Fashion, have created, with ever-changing results that are in sync with the changing
products of Corporate America. Psychologists have pointed out
that the shame of not being cool, which means not being like everybody else, is a stronger sentiment than the pride of ownership. It is
the reason why people who have a lot, or have everything they
need, will still buy more of what's trendy and fashionable, and
thus become Customers again, and again, and again. Such post-

modern realizations that "wants trump needs" and "shame beats pride" has had a fundamental effect on Marketing and its strategic tool, Maslow's Pyramid. Of the pyramid's original five layers the lowest three are called *deficiency needs* or *d-needs*. They are, in other words, still true old-fashioned necessities and are named, from bottom to top: Physiological needs, Security, and Friendship/Belonging. Marketing, and therefore also Customer interest, has moved away from these three bottom layers where the motivation to spend money is small and driven by fixed costs, for instance for food, mortgage, and family. The largest portion of variable discretionary spending has moved to the fourth layer, which can briefly be called *Esteem*. Self-confidence and respect by others come from being like others, which is a direct results of wanting (and buying) what everybody else is buying. That's why iPhones and iPads, Nike sneakers and Starbucks coffee, preshrunk jeans and organic bran cereals have succeeded with Customers, while milk and bread cannot even be taxed.

Most interesting, however, is the modern Customer's spending on wares belonging to the tip of the pyramid – *Self-actualization*. Maslow's theory, and traditional Marketing following him, predicted a dynamic progress of needs from lower to higher – once the lower need was filled, a Customer would move higher and spend his or her money there. This, as we have just seen, is no longer true for the lower layers, since free and voluntary spending is concentrated on layer four – *Esteem*. It is also untrue for the highest layer – *Self-actualization*. Practically no money is spent there, and no Customer interest exists in the components that make up Self-actualization, such as morality, creativity, spontaneity, and lack of prejudice. "Where," a Customer may well cry out, "can I even buy that? In malls? On-line?" In addition, even if you can find these elusive wares, their prices vary, there is no quality control, and there will anyway soon be new versions and updates.

Advertising has long since adjusted. Ads for bread and milk, for instance, are few and far between. On the other hand, Esteem-ware such as electronic gadgets, golf clubs, and perfumes are no longer promoted as things a Customer can buy; "things" have become mere exchangeable contents of ads, and it is essentially *these ads* that a Customer buys. He is attracted by Advertising, not by the product advertised. Advertising has superseded products just as swiftly as wants have supplanted needs.

With this transformation, the Customer has metamorphosed too – into a carrier of Advertising. His walk-in closet stores no garment that doesn't carry a brand label and a visible logo which he wears like a walking billboard: Adidas sneakers, Calvin Klein socks, Jockey shorts, Rolex watches, Yves Saint Laurent ties, Pierre Cardin shirts, Tommy Hilfiger sweaters, Hugo Boss, Gianni Versace, Christian Dior, Gucci, Louis Vuitton, Fendi, and on and on. There he goes to play tennis displaying the Ralph Lauren logo on his shirt, a Wilson tennis racquet in his right hand, a venti-sized Starbucks soy-enhanced organic latte in his left, and on his head a visor with the ubiquitous Nike swoosh.

When Adam and Eve ate the forbidden fruit, they not only knew both good and evil and how to distinguish between them, but they also realized that they were naked. Embarrassed, Eve sewed loincloths for themselves, but for their kids Cain and Abel they eventually went shopping at a store east of Eden. Later, much later, Eve began reading Vogue and shopped at The Gap, and Adam bought a used car at a dealer where the snake, thrown out of paradise, had found gainful employment and greeted her customer with an honest head wiggle: "Nice to see you again!"

The Pundit

A Pundit, also known as a Guru, is an alleged or self-ordained expert. Most political pundits appear on talk radio and cable networks, sitting in a garishly decorated studio where they are treated like experts by the anchors. However, here I am more concerned with the slightly less ephemeral pundit who doesn't only voice off but writes things down, someone who publishes his (or her) opinion, analysis, and commentary in mass media outlets, especially in newspapers and blogs. His readers form a well-defined group, his constituency, his base, which seldom varies. A Pundit knows for whom he's writing, and readers always know what they will get.

A Pundit's areas of commentary is usually one for which no fixed rules exist: politics, business, and culture, because here everything is not only possible but can be claimed to be subjectively true. A Pundit's daily pronouncements are as eclectic as they are non-falsifiable (because they are opinions, not logical arguments). From Socrates, who was also eclectic and not refuted until death finished the argument for him, he differs by the great philosopher's admission, "I know that I don't know." A Pundit who always says more than what he knows will not admit to ignorance because he doesn't know what he doesn't know.

With objective truths and prognostications, such as interest rates, stock market moves, product introductions, customer preferences, the Pundit scores worse than what Seneca (himself a Pundit on Nero's court) requires of an archer:

Sagittarius non aliquando ferire debet, sed aliquando deerrare.

An archer must not just sometimes *hit* the mark; he must *only sometimes miss* it.

It does happen that a Pundit is a scholar or a tenured professor, someone who has new ideas, conducts research, reads books, and is paid for the labor of thinking, like Paul Krugman of the New York Times. In most cases, however, the defining term "expert" has nothing to do with expertise or experience, judgment or insight. Some of the most popular Pundits belly-flopped into the field of punditry after their educational flight ran out of brain fuel. Sean Hannity and Rush Limbaugh dropped out of college. Glenn Beck never got started with college and adopted the "comprehensive worldview" of the Mormon Church instead. Rather than acquiring boring academic knowledge or deeper subject matter expertise or hard-earned job experience, a Pundit has only to form a small set of strong opinions, choose a recognizable vocabulary, select his quotable heroes, and then mix these ingredients into the same old wine in ever new bottles with catchy labels. Because of this universal recipe of predictability, a Pundit will lose his job if he strays from his perceived wholesome image and surprises or disappoints his constituents – which happened to Christopher Buckley, who was fired from his National Review punditry job when he endorsed Obama for president, and to Jeffrey Lord at CNN, when he used a Nazi gesture, and to Bill O'Reilly of Fox News because of harassment suits that the network didn't want to reimburse anymore.

A word about the Pundit's preparation for his appearance on cable network: After eating his cereal and reading the morning papers (his "research"), the Pundit moves from kitchen table to writing table and checks on the Internet what's hot today. He (or she, there are many excellent pundita) chooses a topic, or a point of view, or an odd "nugget" factoid that will please his or her constituency. Maureen Dowd will always say something catty and personal in her cartoonish pieces, criticize Obama for having been not tough enough during his presidency, mention at least one gender issue, and once a year letting her embarrassing brother Kevin spout Breitbart sewage. Her bogeyman used to be Dick Cheney, now it is of course Donald J. Trump. Ann Coulter's crude style is represented by, "We should invade their countries, kill their leaders and convert them to Christianity." Paul Krugman corrects us, quotes facts, and is liberal with the government's money, which needs to be spent so that the benefits of deficits can be explored. Tom Friedman will use the word "global" three times, employ at least two mixed metaphors, and cite one published paper. Gail Collins is like your older, smarter, and funnier sister, refreshingly intelligent and distraught by Trump. David Brooks tries hard to be a progressive, yet deeply Republican Mr. Rogers, but is more avuncular than friendly, and he tries to show periodically how well-read he is, ingredients which together makes for the oxymoron "avuncular educated Republican." And so on, for the fifty top Pundits in this country. And once he or she has written the column or blog for the day? "In the afternoons he is in the habit of going into crowded rooms and making everybody else feel inferior. The evenings are reserved for extended bouts of name-dropping" – as conservative Pundit David Brooks parodied the even more conservative William F. Buckley Jr. in 1983.

The Survivor

"This fellow could not drown." These are Gonzalo's prophetic words about the sinking ship's Boatswain in Shakespeare's play "The Tempest". This fellow is a Survivor.

Some compare his resilience to the force that makes a cork bounce back up from under water. Some just call him a good swimmer. There are also a few detractors who, having themselves once swallowed some water on their own way down, would gladly shoot a torpedo into his ship. Not that his ship is ever grand or an easy target. The Survivor is not the most visible, nor the most sought after employee or manager, but he is not deliberately avoided either. His colleagues realize that a cork has admirable properties and advantages over a rock that's just throwing its weight around. When the Survivor is in luck and on top, he does favors for people, puts in a good word for them, and lends them a hand, even money.

Surviving adversities has strengthened his ego, and Fate must surely have meant him to be strong. When old Gonzalo calls to the Boatswain / Survivor: "... remember whom thou hast aboard," the latter confidently answers, "None that I more love than myself."

Sure – the Survivor has made his mistakes. He has at times shown a slump in his enthusiasm, and he has deliberately kept his head down during rougher goings. So what if he does submerge temporarily? It is never longer than it takes to weather a storm. Swallowing the salty water of a bad performance review or stranding his career boat on the cliff of dead-end jobs while more talented colleagues steam ahead doesn't make him a Has-been. When the winds change and the tide comes in to raise his ship, he sets his sails again for the next journey: the Survivor is back.

You cannot count on luck alone, not even as a Survivor. Not always will the fortuitous force of buoyancy pop you back up to the surface. Nor can you count on Noah to invite you to a berth on his ark, when the gods are angry and dark clouds bespeak a coming reorg or lay-off. The true Survivor takes the smallest hint when he hears about the weather changing, and when the rain drops are starting to fall he is already sitting pretty, warm and dry, deep in the belly of Noah's boat – as a stowaway. (He always knows when there is an opening in another division where he can hide while the storm passes.) But when the dove comes back with an olive leaf in her beak as proof that the dark clouds have blown away, he is quickly back on his feet to disembark and look if the leaf came from a tree that has some olives and pistachio nuts left for him.

With the deluge over and the land dry again, he knows that having to cultivate his own garden again – proving himself anew – takes much energy, perhaps even the exertion of learning another skill and finding a new job. The Survivor has provided for this situation long ago. Now he cashes in on the favors he did for others when he was lucky and on top. And so he gets another position, without too much effort.

His means of transportation from position to position is the bandwagon pulled by men who are more dynamic than him. Instinctively he recognizes the vehicles on which he can hitch a ride, as he did with the ark. As mentioned above, he may well have been a stowaway during the Big Flood. But isn't it more likely that he knew Noah, and that Noah knew him? Noah was God's Fair-Haired Boy, and the Survivor must have helped him as a friend in the past. And would Noah let down a friend? No; no more than the powerful Magus Prospero would let down the Boatswain. The ship, destroyed by the tempest in Act I, is, as we reach Act V, "tight and yare [i.e., ready] and bravely rigg'd as when / We first put out to sea." Again, the Survivor is back.

Literary men and women have called the Survivor the Mr. Micawber of the corporation, after the fictional character in Charles Dickens's novel David Copperfield. For us normal readers the

Merriam-Webster Dictionary defines a Micawber as "one who is poor but lives in optimistic expectation of better fortune."

The Trophy Wife

Grammatically, "wife" is singular, and so are the words "pair" and "portmanteau." In a corporate setting, however, and in particular for the successful corporate man, a wife often shares the pluralized meaning of "pair" and "portmanteau" in her own way. This calls for further explanations.

In the beginning, a corporate man and his wife are a couple like many others, engaged in the usual bond of matrimony, monogamous and mostly monotonous mating. They are a twosome, belonging together like a pair of socks. Of course the story doesn't have to end there. The portmanteau comes into play.

A portmanteau word packs together the meaning of two words into a new one whose meaning is a combination of its parts. Thus, as Humpty Dumpty teaches Alice, the portmanteau adjective "slithy" is a merger of the word "lithe" (which according to Humpty Dumpty's dictionary means active, but which Webster's Dictionary also explains as gentle and flexible) and the word "slimy." With Humpty Dumpty's mixing recipe in mind, we know exactly what a "slithy salesman" or a "slithy congressman" is. Similarly, the Corporate Wife is a blend of two different concepts, indeed of two distinct realities.

There is first the active woman who bears children for the corporate man, her husband. She patiently carries the burden of his corporate career through lonely evenings and lowly pay. She distinguishes herself by unglamorous persistence and by an unending belief in her husband. She adapts to the vagaries of success and failure, enjoys his raises and shares his disappointments. This sympathetic flexibility is her undoing. Her life will become "mimsy," at once miserable in its outlook and flimsy in its purpose.

Once her corporate husband has risen a few steps up the corporate ladder, where "job" and "work" appear only as the lowest rungs leading to higher platforms such as "career," and "position," he starts to believe in himself so much that he'll want to add to the un-glamorous status quo at home a more amorous existence – he wants to add a mistress. On first impulse he may wish to repeal his marriage and replace his childbearing wife with an alternative who can demonstrate his business savvy by showing a sassy front and sexy back – a trophy wife! Weighing the pros and cons, however, he prefers to have, hold, and keep them both, the practical home-maker and mother of his children, AND his paramour for making love and mothering him. But usually even Mister Corporate Macho has to settle for one or the other, sooner or later, and may end up with none.

Here are the possible scenarios for her and for him. After getting wind of his affair, the first wife is frumious[1], of course; but after de-nial, pain, fury, depression, adjustment, and acceptance, she real-izes she's no Clytemnestra who'd murder her husband Agamem-non, but neither is she a Penelope who'll wait for her Ulysses to come back home after twenty years of detours and enchantments with his trophy Circe. So she changes her mimsy life and finds her own Robert-Kincaid-Clint-Eastwood who ravishes her on a rickety bridge in Madison County. Or she moves in with a kind and ma-ture widower, an old friend who takes Flomax, but who also gladly accompanies her to the symphony. They go in her car, a black Mer-cedes or silver Jaguar, because now in the autumn of her life, her prenuptial agreement with her faithless corporate husband has be-come more important than a postmortem last will and testament,

---

1 Frumious: In the preface to *The Hunting of the Snark*, Carroll defines 'frumious' as follows:

"Take the two words 'fuming' and 'furious'. Make up your mind that you will say both words, but leave it unsettled which you will say first. Now open your mouth and speak. If your thoughts incline ever so little towards 'fuming', you will say 'fuming-furious'; if they turn, by even a hair's breadth, towards 'furious', you will say 'furious-fuming'; but if you have the rarest of gifts, a perfectly balanced mind, you will say 'frumious'."

which may only have gotten her, as it did Shakespeare's wife Anne Hathaway, his second-best bed.

And the corporate man himself? As soon as his luck runs out and his corporate fortune sags like the flesh on his chin, he will be alone in his love nest

Hung with the trophies of my lovers gone,

as Shakespeare writes in Sonnet 31, and he may soon see his frabjous[2] Circe with a younger MBA from the Wharton School of Business, or another strapping Fair-Haired Boy from the Sales department who drives a BMW, calls her on his iPhone, tweets like a bird of paradise, exercises regularly, eats salad and tofu, drinks white wine, and is, for Circe, the ideal boy toy, because "his leg excels all men's" (according to the Nurse's words to Juliet about Romeo's body, see "Romeo and Juliet," Act II, scene 5).

In the end, Circe too, is cast aside and left somewhere on a shelf of memories, now only an embarrassing leftover that is reminiscent, like all shining trophies from the past, of younger and more foolish days.

---

2   Frabjous: fabulous and joyous

I
Advanced Characters

The Corporate Spirit

A triumvirate governs the fate of a company: the Chairman of the Board, the CEO, and the Corporate Spirit. You cannot drink this Spirit; but you can imbibe it metaphorically so that you, too, can become a true believer.

The Corporate Spirit is the essence of the carefully crafted, or organically grown, Corporate Culture that upper management wants the lower echelons to subscribe to and live by. Not always carved in stone as in Moses's tablets, but more often copied on heavy paper, the Corporate Spirit is distributed into cubicles from Corporate Hill as if it came from Mount Sinai. In practice, it appears in the two forms of (1) commandments or Corporate Objectives, such as *What Thou Shalt or Shall Not Do for the company*, and of (2) moral imperatives or Company Values, for instance *How Thou Shalt Behave in the Company*.

In addition to these sacred texts, corporations often have a profane Employee Handbook, in which the daily interactions of employees are regulated like traffic rules out of DMV pamphlets, together with penalties for infractions. An example from an early handbook reads like this:

"If an employee digs a well and doesn't cover it, and an ox or a donkey falls into it, the proprietor of said well shall pay full damages to the owner of the animal, and the dead animal shall belong to him" (Exodus 21:33; Old Testament).

A more recent text states:

"f you call your fellow employee an idiot, you are in danger of being brought before the court. And if you curse him, you are in danger of the fires of hell" (Matthew 5:21; New Testament).

But let's return to the Corporate Spirit and look more closely at the practical commandments, or Corporate Objectives.

Up towards the end of the 20th century, practically all corporations had Profit as the # 1 objective, because that's a capitalist no-brainer. Towards the end of the list of Objectives came something about "Commitment to our employees." Since the beginning of the 21st century most corporations have adjusted and put as # 1 the (lip) service to their customers, stressing things like "Customer Loyalty" or the sugary "Delighting Our Customers," while Profit has fallen to #2, while at the end of the list there's still something about "Commitment to our Employees."

As to Values, a decade ago honesty (or one of its synonyms) was top. Now even here the profit-producing Customer, a mythical giant who's present everywhere and visible nowhere, has moved to the top: "Passion for Customers" was at one time #1 on Hewlett-Packard's list of "Our Shared Values," and the last item was the bloated term "Uncompromising integrity." The value of integrity and the objective of commitment to employees will, however, be subjected to the imperative of Profit and therefore lead to layoffs. Such a compromise has internally been called the New HP Way. Similarly, last we checked, IBM had as its #1 value "Dedication to every client's success" and as their last one "Trust". Or compare Goldman Sachs's Business Principles, with the last one (#14) offering the double whammy "Integrity and honesty." Google is a bit more original, listing in a brag list "Ten things we know to be true," among which you'll find the advertiser's credo "You can make money without doing evil." AIG doesn't publish ethical guidelines *per se*, but does flaunt a "Luxury Expenditure Policy." Halliburton has a touchingly phrased Human Rights Policy Statement ("We have long addressed our belief in human dignity, human rights, and fairness ...") and encourages the democratic process with uncompromising frankness: "When permitted by law and authorized by the Chief Executive Officer, expenditures of Company funds may be made to inform or influence the voting public on an issue of importance to the business of the Company and its shareholders."

There are many other ways in which corporations give advice as to what you should do and believe, so that your life has purpose and direction. After all, faith, purpose, and direction: that's what the Corporate Spirit is all about!

The Corporate Spirit will not tell you what the company will do for you (salary, security, sense of importance and similar superficialities), but only what you can do for the company. The Corporate Spirit offers food for (positive) thought, but not plain bread and butter. And even if you had your daily loaf of bread and bi-weekly paycheck: No man or woman can live on bread alone. Men and women need more. They need spiritual support. It is in this vein that we may compare the Corporate Spirit to a jockstrap or a bra. Neither is absolutely necessary when the tide is low and the going is slow. But when we need to perform as business warriors in sales demonstrations, when we are out in the battle-fields to create demands for our products where there is none, when we pitch our wares where they are not needed: it is then that the Corporate Spirit holds us up!

The Corporation as a Person

Yes, the American Corporation is a person, a so-called legal or artificial person. It has many of the rights, responsibilities, privileges, liabilities, and faults a natural person like you and I have. The founders and framers of the U.S. Constitution apparently did not know this, but many people, CEOs and Supreme Justices among them, believe that endowing a Corporation with personhood was implicitly intended all along in order to create a *better* "person". After all, you and I have proven, since paradise was lost, to be defective and disappointing. No wonder that Corporations are more popular, and treated better by the taxman, than your average person in the street.

To begin with, being a person, a Corporation can make and break contracts, sue and be sued, have debts and own property, pay and avoid taxes. A Corporation is also a citizen (of the State where it was incorporated) and will therefore be able to travel abroad, e.g., to the Cayman Islands.

But a Corporation is more than an artificial being; it has human rights, constitutional rights. This is how it came about:

Go back to 1886, to the Supreme Court case *Santa Clara County v. Southern Pacific Railroad*. Before oral arguments started, Chief Justice Morrison R. Waite said, within earshot of a court reporter named J.C. Bancroft Davis, to the attorneys that were lollygagging about that he didn't want to hear any arguments about whether the provisions of the Fourteenth Amendment, which forbids any State to deny "any person" within its jurisdiction "the equal protection of the laws," apply to corporations, closing with the fateful assertion, "We are all of the opinion that it does."

Ever since this reporter, J.C. Bancroft Davis, put Justice Waite's pretrial chit-chat on record, courts have acted as if the quip represented a legally binding precedent. The only issue, up to this day, is how far this "equal protection" clause in the Fourteenth Amendment (whose original purpose was to protect freed slaves!) may extend in the case of corporations. Can corporations keep and bear firearms? Concealed ones, too? Can a Corporation take "the Fifth" so that it shall it not "be compelled in any criminal case to be a witness against" itself? And is there double jeopardy for corporations?

The biggest achievement to fully include a Corporation in the Bill of Rights was made on January 21, 2010. On this day in history, the Supreme Court issued a ruling in *Citizens United v. Federal Election Commission* that not only affirmed but expanded corporate First Amendment rights to free speech in elections, a "speech" that may also mean the "right" to splurge potentially unlimited campaign contributions upon corporation-friendly candidates – plus any amount of money spent to discredit the other side. As the saying goes: "Money speaks." And it has a loud voice.

Remarkable in this kowtow to the American Corporation is (1) that the Court reversed its own 2003 decision in *McConnell v. Federal Election Commission*, and (2) rendered a decision far more expansive than the litigants originally sought. It's so easy legally to make an Angel out of Lucifer.

There exist still a few regrettable exceptions for full legal personhood of a Corporation. It is, for instance, currently not possible for two corporations to get married. That is a shame, because a simple marriage, preferably in a church, would simplify what is now a complicated and costly process of the civil union of mergers and acquisitions. Furthermore, corporations still cannot vote in elections. If they could – and the Roberts-Court appears to be reviewing this as an Amendment XV issue through self-initiated *writ of certiorari* – the old-fashioned principle of Chief Justice Earl Warren, "one man, one vote," would be replaced by a new principle that replaces "one man" by the number of shares he owns (which is already practiced *within* corporations).

So far it has not been possible for a Corporation to be elected into public office. Most glaringly, so far a Corporation cannot become the POTUS, President Of The United States. The opinion that such a formal election and swearing-in hasn't been necessary, because big corporations in the insurance, oil, and banking industries (to name a few) have already, through their lobbyist and other well-greased connections, attained all the power, not only in the executive, but also in the legislative and legal branches of government – well, that fact is no excuse. A Corporation, as a person endowed with more and more rights, must not shirk the responsibility and, as a good citizen, be ready to serve the people it sells its products to.

Little did we know until the 45th president short-circuited the drive of a corporation becoming POTUS. We didn't need an entity with bylaws, shareholders, quarterly reporting, and other openly visible aspects that, by law, a Corporation as a "public" person has to show. It is enough that a natural person, sufficiently vulgar and incompetent, would parlay his father's money into a brand known for advertising sleazy excess and make-believe luxury, and finagle family and rich cronies to declare him POTUS-CEO with corporate headquarters at the White House.

CorpSpeak

CorpSpeak is the voice of the Corporate Spirit, it is the vernacular of the company philosophy. CorpSpeak is not, however, a fully developed language. It is the stump of a lingo, a glorified jargon of an in-group. If you speak it, you belong. If you don't, you don't. It has been noticed by outside observers that although the vocabulary of CorpSpeak changes almost daily, the size of its dictionary and the number of grammatical rules are decreasing every year. This feat is achieved, for instance, by euphemistic reformulations that get rid of certain words and word combinations. A quarterly loss is simply called negative profit; reducing the workforce by firing people is more easily called rightsizing; negatively charged words such as "problem," difficulty," and "issue" are replaced by the single, positive and chivalrous sounding term "challenge" or "opportunity"– and so forth. Adverbs are also avoided where adjectives will do, as in "His bullet points were real interesting," or "Lemme say it loud and clear, we need to do this quick."

The linguistic treats of CorpSpeak do not open up new avenues of eloquence. Instead, we are talking grammatical, literal, and even cerebral handicap here whenever you partake in GroupSpeak and therefore also in GroupThink. Making this sacrifice is the price of belonging to the brotherhood of CorpSpeakers. If style is a characteristic sound that words make in the human mind, then CorpSpeak will invoke in your head the painful shriek of keying an old Chevy.

Passing from stylistic to phenomenological assessment, CorpSpeak is easily detected by the high frequency of acronyms sprinkled throughout its body of speech. These are not only dusty specimens like ASAP and FYI, IT and R&D, FTE and FTO, but also relative newcomers such as LBO (Leveraged Buy-Out) and MBWA (Managing By Walking Around), cutesy phrases like "lol", "Tks" and thousands of combinations of letters meaningful only to the computer-fully-literate.

At the grammatical level, split infinitives are popular with Corp-Speakers and used to better glue together a pretentious beginning with a pointless ending of a sentence. The deep structure, if there is any, reveals a strutting and posturing that would put to shame an entire farm of roosters, while Saussurean semantics shows CorpSpeak to be only half as vigorous as the etiolated scholar in George Eliot's novel Middlemarch. All of this highbrow stuff has been treated in academic dissertations at Harvard and the Wharton School of Business.

Following Orwell's example of Newspeak, the CorpSpeak's dictionary can be divided into three vocabularies.

The *A vocabulary* consists of words needed for everyday business communication. It is therefore made up mainly of buzzwords and clichés. These express simple, but fuzzy and rather large concepts and phrases that are the unquestioned base and *lingua franca* of elementary CorpSpeak. Examples are: the buck stops here, challenge (instead of problem), leverage, give a heads-up, customer satisfaction (or even the preposterous phrase "delighting the customer"), total quality focus, hotbed, utilize, effective, framework, touch-and-feel, take-away, bottom line, in a timely manner, wordsmithing a memo, facilitating a meeting, peeling the onion, the devil is in the details, and so on – mostly harmless fillers and meaningless buffers: "At the end of the day, it's a team effort to proactively drive the remaining issues and to cost-efficiently implement the strategies and tactics as laid out in the business plan ..."

Included in the *B vocabulary*, by contrast, are words that have been deliberately constructed for ideological purposes. They are intended to impose a desirable mental attitude. Most of them are long words or composite phrases characteristic of a postmodern industry: involuntary severance benefits package, pro-active engagement, competitive advantage, downsizing and aligning, reorganization and focus on the core competencies, profit sharing, empowerment seminars, company values, leadership through quality and service, and so on -- mostly with a positive and faintly pedagogical connotation. Typical are also neologisms and metaphors that tend to contain an explicit or implied criticism, judgment, exhortation, or threat. Examples are vapor ware, blamestorming, administrivia, Quality First, back of the envelope calculation, and many more.

Finally, the C *vocabulary* consists of scientific terms and technical jargon, varying by different industry sectors and specialties: macro and micro economics, hardware and software, hi tech, chip, interface, book value, P/E ratio, franchising, peripherals, plug-compatible, mainframe, a viral (web-) site, crowd sourcing, cloud computing, long tail marketing, and thousands more.

Ezra Pound has summarized CorpSpeak in Cantos XIV:

(...)
the perverts, the perverters of language,
the perverts, who have set money-lust
Before the pleasures of the senses;
howling, as of a hen-yard in a printing-house,
the clatter of presses,
the blowing of dry dust and stray paper,
foetor, sweat, the stench of stale oranges,
(...)

Profit

"In All Labor There is Profit." (Proverbs 14:23)

Profit, although fickle and sometimes endowed with feminine gender ("she" instead of "it"), is still the noblest of all Corporate Characters, the diva on Wall Street and the beloved star of every investor. The corporate show can't go on without her for very long, or without her supporting cast, Sales and Revenues. She is often distracted and upset by her ugly step-sisters Expense and Cost-of-Sales, both of whom are green with envy and try to pull her down with their negativism. In spite of such dysfunctional family relations, it's her, Profit, who is exposed every quarter in the limelight of Wall Street's center stage, where she must strut her stuff and show her numbers to analysts and stock brokers. Seeing a pretty Profit, they exclaim: "Isn't a stock trading corporation the most ingenious device for all of us to make individual profit without individual responsibility?"

In medical terms, Profit and her understudy, the shareholder's Dividends, are Wall Street's short term indicators of a company's health. Wall Street encourages us to take red cheeks as proof for physical well-being.

It is sometimes forgotten that neither Forbes nor the editors of the Wall Street Journal are the theoreticians of Profit. Early Too-Good-To-Be-True theories of Profit have tried to imitate popes who sold indulgences at a high price and at no cost. But aside from these early over-optimistic pioneers of practical profiteers, the historic honor of outstanding profit theoretician goes to Karl Marx. For him, Profit was the newfangled cousin of what he had initially called "surplus value," an awkward translation of the German word "Mehrwert," which literally means "more value". More than what? More than what you deserve? More than what you earned? More than enough? No; quite simply put, surplus value is the difference between what a company takes in for its products and what it pays out for making them. Critics have argued that the equation "surplus value = price minus labor cost and other expenses" is frivolously simple. Which may well be true: Advertising, packaging, executive bonuses, and litigation are of much higher priority in the Profit calculus than, say, the relatively insignificant budget for salaries.

Thoreau, born a year before Marx, applied Marx's terminology. He called his annual expenses "my outgoes" (which amounted to $14.72 1/2). After having accumulated an income of $23.44 – mainly from selling beans – he made "a pecuniary profit" (his very words) of $8.71 1/2. Corporate executives never grow tired of pointing out from this classical example how such a profit margin of 37% can be obtained only if the wages are kept low.

A recently hired supernumerary on the Profit show is the term "value added," as in "value added retailers" or VARs. They are, in essence, the old go-betweens or middle men who don't add to, but subtract from the Profit by taking their piece of the pie up-front. To understand this, think of a go-between who, as the reward of his matchmaking services, sleeps with the bride.

The antonym to Profit is every CEO's nightmare: Negative Profit, also known as Loss. Profit shows because of good management. Loss appears despite good management.

Corporate Humor

There is one overriding axiom ruling the theory and practice of corporate behavior: *No Surprises!* This terse maxim applies to Corporate Humor in particular.

The taxonomy of corporate humor distinguishes between two classes of jokes. There is, first, the unsystematic, spontaneous, often involuntary one-liner, which is preferred by management because its delivery takes little time. Examples are the managerial quip, describing tough managerial project reviews as "rectal exams." Or the naive question of an interviewee, "Does your company's life insurance cover suicide?" Or take the buxom secretary who's handing her ogling boss two butterscotch candies, asking, "Are those your eyeballs? I found them in my cleavage."

Depending on where and who you are, you are advised to use your one-line drollery wisely and in a job-related manner. A support representative may lighten the tension with an uptight customer through some well-placed sarcasm and then add, "Sarcasm is just one more service we offer." Generally, the spectrum of eligible quick-mirth ranges from "delightfully deprecatory" (regarding your own accomplishments) to "severely adulatory" (regarding your boss's achievements). The implied joke is that you think all the time that the opposite is true – sort of like irony, but not really, because your boss takes your flattery seriously.

Second is the systematic, planned, deliberate jesting that executives display in official speeches to large assemblies of employees. The public art of official comedy can only be learned in week-long humor workshops, where humor consultants teach managers how to inject humor in an otherwise humorless office environment. He comes with handouts that ask his students "to be prepared to giggle," then introduces himself by saying, "I don't work here. I'm a consultant," adding quickly and with perfect timing, "Just kidding," whereupon his audience is completely baffled.

A professional humor consultant approaches his or her task scientifically. This science is in many cases based on the research done by Professor Melanie Booth-Butterfield of West Virginia University. She summarizes the result of extensive humor research in the following funny way on her website, "We've found that producing effective humor is an individual difference (measured by the Humor Orientation scale) and that people who are high on humor orientation (High HOs) are observably funnier than those who score low on the scale." The scale refers to a sophisticated self-test where you rate your gut response to propositions such as "I can be funny without having to rehearse a joke" on a scale from "strongly agree" to "strongly disagree."

There are humor consultants paid by corporations, and there are humorous columnists paying homage to corporations. An intellectual version (sometimes called "Princeton Edition") of Corporate Humor is regularly put on show by the comedian George F. Will, Ph.D. His spontaneity of expression and simplicity of style are equaled only by his touching sympathy for the American corporation and lower taxes. Dr. Will has made comical statements about global warming, and his many uproarious quotes taken from dead writers, his facial expression, mannerisms and bow tie make him a real and believable clown.

Higher forms of humor such as parody, satire, irony and puns are considered dangerously close to lèse majesté, an offense to the straitlaced Corporate Spirit. That's why departmental memos are just as funny as the Old Testament. Practical jokes and tasteless pranks, scatological wit, and viewing funny soft porn with Jodie Fisher ("Intimate Obsession," "Body of Influence 2") are reserved for vice-presidents and CEOs. Guffaws were recently heard from a boardroom when the elderly chairman asked his assistant Maureen for help with a new fax machine with the words, "My equipment is so old, it takes forever to finish."

Much corporate amusement is also derived from "making fun" of people, as in the following story where sales guys show up an engineer:

A group of sales guys were given the assignment of measuring the height of a flagpole. In suit and tie, they march out to the flagpole with their ladders and tape measures, falling all over themselves to get an accurate reading. An engineer comes along and sees what they're trying to do. He walks over, pulls the flagpole out of the ground, lays it flat, measures it from end to end, gives the measurement to the head salesmen and walks away.

After the engineer has gone, the head salesman turns to the other sales people and laughs, "Isn't that just like an engineer?!" he says, "we're looking for the height, and he gives us the length!"

The ROI or Return On Investment

Imagine a candy machine: You put a couple of coins into the slot, choose, and press a button, after which the machine makes a few chugging noises, and with a plop your choice of candy drops into the trough from where you retrieve your loot. This candy machine is a fair analogy and a telltale example for the ROI, the return on investment. An input, your invested coins, triggers a mechanism that returns the desired treat.

Why is it a telltale example? If only it were so simple! For one thing (we've all experienced it), the machine may simply swallow your coins and sit there, a stubborn and idle mechanism, even if you talk to it and, when that doesn't help, beat it with your fists. Sometimes, although rarely, you press for a Mars bar and what drops down is a bag of Gummi Bears. More often, the candy bar is disappointing – stale, dried up, too sweet, too small, too unhealthy, and, when you think about it, not worth your investment. The true art of the ROI consists in the trick of returning something of *higher* value from a *lesser* investment, like turning an invested bottle of water into wine.

The more likely input-output scenario for an ROI is "Tit for tat," or "You get (only) what you paid for." In this general form, the ROI is a concept that transcends corporate life and touches yours and mine. We all wish, however, for a little more than just at tit for a tat, and hope for a bonus. For instance: A "good" school (a private grammar school or a name-brand university) will cost you a pretty penny. Tuition, fees, room and board are what you invest for Johnny, your first-born. Let's say you pay for Johnny to become a lawyer. If after many years, on graduation day, you get back only a poet, you may be inclined to phone the dean and the bursar, or the Better Business Bureau, and demand your money back. In your opinion, you didn't get back what you paid for.

On the other hand, when Johnny graduates into a professional football player or a hedge fund manager, then you have invested your money wisely and you'll no doubt continue to believe in the value of an education. Your parental gratefulness might even exceed your business satisfaction, so that in a weak and emotional moment you may lose control and send to the bursar of Johnny's *alma mater* a hefty check intended to help with the new sports arena or business school library. In addition to showing your appreciation regarding Johnny, all that you personally would like in return for your gift is a voice in the hiring of the new coach or quarterback.

These almost philosophical considerations suggest that the nexus between the I and the R of ROI is not only a logical but also a causal one. Take any corporation, where the I is usually money plus the employees' skills, just as fire, coal, and water are the investments in a steam engine. The movement of the locomotion, the R, is caused by the pressure of water heated by coal fire. By the same token the burnout of employees, fired up by money, causes the corporation to move forward.

Your handling of the ROI will determine your ultimate niche in Corporate America. Asking too much I while regurgitating too little R will soon demote you to a Has-Been. The only entities where the equations

I = BIG and

R = SMALL

are permitted to hold simultaneously true are government sponsored R&D labs and Congress. On the other hand, when you can finagle a big R from a small I, you will make a career as the Fair-Haired Boy of shareholders. The Visionary, meanwhile, assumes that the I will come from anywhere and produce the R, not now but sometime.

At the end of your life, you will learn about the ultimate ROI. On that late and final day, God will weigh your life's return against the lump of clay he invested in you long ago on that sixth day when he created you. Based on this R and this I, he will make his judgment.

Gossip

"Love and a cough cannot be hid," wrote the poetic priest George Herbert in 1651. To these two old afflictions, according to corporate wisdom, should be added Gossip. Pharmacists recommend syrups against the cough, but they have no medication against falling in love, and neither aspirin nor electroshock therapy are cures for gossip. Love and gossip are deeply rooted in human nature, the first one in the urge to cohabitate and copulate, and the second in the urge to congregate and communicate. In order to prevent Gossip from becoming too disturbing, like the common cough, it is best to cover your mouth. This prophylactic measure should be applied not simply by your hands (behind which you can still whisper), but by closing your lips tightly before another piece of Gossip can get out.

Gossip is always around, anytime, anyplace. It is almost like a kind of divinity, according to Homer. In corporations, there exist several official occasions encouraging Gossip. One is called "business luncheon," where the readiness for Gossip is signaled in advance by the casual "Let's do lunch sometime." A luncheon provides also an opportunity to lay down a particular type of humus upon which true Gossip can grow: the deliberate Rumor. If such a fertile Rumor is generated successfully, the business luncheon is called a "power lunch." On these or other Gossip-facilitating occasions, when behind Chardonnay glasses serious gabbing takes place, male chattiness does not have to take second place to the more notorious but often less vicious gossip performed by women. Female Gossip fills the room, including the restroom, but male Gossip can kill careers: "You know Johnson in Sales? Well, his numbers are, you know, just between you and me ..."

The purpose of Gossip is not primarily the exchange of the kind of information that is not regularly found on a company's public bulletin board. It is truly a higher form of communication. Not only binary bits and bytes of factual messages are exchanged over gossipy channels, but bits and pieces of personal reckoning. "And we two will rail against our mistress, our manager, the world, and all our misery," as we read in Shakespeare's "As You Like It."

Rarely (and this adds to its allurement) does Gossip stress the positive, and never (this adds to timeliness) is it about the future. The body of Gossip consists of trivial but juicy tidbits of unofficial factoids that have their roots in real or imagined events of the past and present. From these roots, Gossip grows like a tree of make-believe knowledge whose fruit may later poison the future.

Deeper down, a person who has eaten from this tree is vying for approval. A Gossip professional is campaigning for his own opinions, which after all have been carefully groomed through long hours of frustrations and misgivings. The more playful amateur Gossip is simply cultivating the vicious art of snooping and delighting in being mischievous.

Mischievous yes, but not aggressive. Modifying another pithy proverb from George Herbert's collection "Jacula Prudentum," we may say "Gossip's bark is worse than its bite." Not directing its arrows against anybody specific, Gossip works more like spraying the bitter juice of magic flowers indiscriminately like Puck in Midsummer Night's Dream.

We must also not forget that it takes at least two to gossip. Ogden Nash had it right:

> There are two kinds of people who blow through life like a breeze,
> And one kind is gossipers, and the other kind is gossipees.
> And they certainly annoy each other,
> But they certainly enjoy each other,
> Yes, they pretend to flout each other,
> But they couldn't do without each other ...

Corporate Romance

If lust is thunder and lightening after a red hot and humid day, if friendship is a warm late-summer evening enjoyed while drinking chamomile tea, then Romance is the sudden arrival of crocus blossoms on a day when the hummingbirds return. And love, compared to stormy lust, brings soothingly good weather, as we read in "Venus and Adonis" II, 799-800:

> Love comforteth, like sunshine after rain,
> But lust's effect is tempest after sun.

At the onset of a Corporate Romance it is not blossoms and hummingbirds that arrive, but more likely a tweet from a computer in the next cubicle, or a text message on your cell, or a bland message asking you to become a friend on the facebook page of your admirer. Such messages contain acronyms and emoticons, which you're expected to understand if you want to partake in a Corporate Romance. Let's say he sends the message "U LOOK GR8 2DAY ;-)", which of course says, with a wink, that you look great today. Immediately, you text your girlfriend in Sales who's your BFF (best friend forever) that, Oh my God, you're *soooo* happy you could cry: "OMG IM SOOOO :'-)". And your friend in Sales may just gape with admiration or jealousy :-O or have a warning: "IMNSHO HES A TWEEDLER" – In my not so humble opinion, he's a computer geek.

It is usually not the best idea to text back immediately that you love him too, as in "ILY2", because that might elicit a scowling " :-X LOL", the latter being an ambiguous Internet slang that usually does not mean you're the Love Of his Life, but rather anything from Laughing Out Loud, Loser On Line, Leg of Lamb or Little Old Lady.

Speaking of the L-word: Love is a venerable English word that is occasionally used even today, mainly in adolescent pop songs, chick flicks, and in advertising ("Love. It's What Makes a Subaru, a

Subaru."). In the past, towards the end of the 16th century, when Shakespeare reigned supreme over the English language, we meet the nimble-footed pair of Woo and Flirt (1583). The active wooer is more often the man, as in

> She's beautiful, and therefore to be woo'd,
> She is a woman, therefore to be won,

in King Henry VI. Flirt has often a more feminine air, meaning then, as it does now "to move erratically, to behave amorously without serious intent" (Webster's). Romeo and Juliet were, in the first phase of their tragic love, a prime example of this lighter, flirty, sentiment.

At around the same time, Love pure was joined by Love Apple (1578), Love Affair (1591), and Lovelock (1592), which refers to a lock of hair hanging sentimentally by itself, separate from the rest. Shakespeare also witnessed the birth of two other terms that would henceforth accompany Flirt and Love: Sex, beginning with Sexless (1598) all the way to Virtual Sex (1992) and Lust, as in Lustihood (since 1599):

> Reason and respect make livers pale and lustihood deject.

(Troilus and Cressida, II,2). The ambivalence and shame of fierce (and secret?) lovemaking, also of nausea and ecstasy (not uncommon even in a modern Corporation when romance is no longer enough), was foreshadowed by the Bard's bawdy Sonnet 129:

> "The expense of spirit in a waste of shame
> Is lust in action; and till in action, lust
> Is perjured, murderous, bloody, full of blame,
> Savage, extreme, rude, cruel, not to trust,
> (…)"

Readers who need to learn more about the ways Shakespeare experienced, and treated in his plays and poems, the emergence of Corporate Romance in Stratford, London and environs, may do well to consult Stanley Wells' book *Shakespeare, Sex, and Love*.

Let's continue with the true goal of Corporate Romance, i. e., Sex. The victorious march of Sex began innocently enough with the Sextuple in 1632, sixteen years after Shakespeare's death, and continued with Sexagesimal (1685), Sexagenarian (1738), and Sexual Intercourse (1799) – we are now in the high classics of Goethe and on our way to Schopenhauer and Byron. Next steps include Sexualize (1839: the Romantics), Sex Appeal & Sexy (1925: the aftershocks of Woodrow Wilson's New Deal), the portmanteau Sexploitation (1942), Sex Kitten (1958: the Cold War), then the climax of this development: Sexism in the 1960's. After that came the necessary corrective of aggressive sex-negative feminism. And finally, Nancy Reagan's directive: Just say No.

What interrupted the progress of Sex? It wasn't just Nancy Reagan. It was the Personal Computer revolution of the 70's and 80's. It upended the sexual revolution of the sixties and seventies. The shift is particularly visible in the nerdy vocabulary of Corporate Romance. What was a simple kiss in the sixties is now seen as the application of a sophisticated interface; a girl's pretty face has become a transparent front-end; light petting has been upgraded to the heavier touch-and-feel.

In addition, the days (or nights) when a Boss looked sweet upon his employee who, bewitched by the attention from above, would let business as usual become unusual monkey business – those days are over, thank goodness. Unwelcome advances and love-trading for favors have rightly been ostracized and branded with two extremely ugly words: sexual harassment, and impeachment. Both the lighter flirt and the heavier infatuation, even among equal employees, interfere with office work and corporate values – as determined by the rules of business conduct, as enshrined in the Employee Handbook.

No wonder that the practice of Corporate Romance is currently going through some advanced emotional re-engineering. We will revisit this topic in a future edition of Corporate Characters, in the vain hope that yet again crocus blossoms will arrive and the hummingbirds will return.

The Business Trip

There are seven "firsts" that shape a man's life in the USA: the first baseball bat, the first love, the first job, the first car, the first wife, the first child, the first divorce. For the business man, there exists yet another rite of passage, equal to baptism in its function to endow you with the sacrament of belonging: the first Business Trip. Tell me what business trip you are on and I'll tell you where you rank in your company.

We recognize the man on a Business Trip already at the check-in counter. Accompanied by their carry-on luggage: Travelpro ($149.99), Samsonite (199.99), or Tumi ($369.99), business travelers carry the grave expression of self-importance on their unsmiling faces. They sport the proud look of pretension and weariness, "Look, man, I got to do this every day; it's hard, but I love it."

Contrary to what you may have learned in school, there are more species alive under the genus of *homo erectus* than just *homo sapiens*. One of these species is the Business Man. Within this very species there exist several sub-species of business trippers. You'll see the battered carry-on bags carried out of the first-class airport lounge by the veteran with the Humphrey Bogart face. He has all but forgotten why he is traveling, or where – as long as the whiskey is good and plenty. You'll also notice the smart attaché case of the clean-shaven traveler, recently promoted to middle manager, who carries a suit-bag of genuine leather and reads the Wall Street Journal while standing in line for business class check-in. He still flaunts his frequent-flier card too openly to be acceptable in the club of true veterans. He is not yet hard-boiled and cynical, but clean and efficient. In his effort to appear cool, he tries to pull a Clint Eastwood and only manages a Michael Douglas. The tight muscles around his chin betray signs of his one great ambition: to travel first class next time.

And then there is the first-timer in his Peter Falk Colombo suit. He still uses a suitcase (it gets lost sometimes) and a square carry-on that doesn't fit under the seat because he travels economy class. Boarding the plane, he slowly makes his way through the first class and the business class sections to the rear of the plane. Once he has found his narrow seat next to drooling babies, backpacking students, and elderly ladies who want to talk to him, he is the only honest man on the plane. He would rather be at home with wife and kids and a beer and watch a game on TV.

Once in his seat, the veteran doesn't eat; he drinks two scotch, stretches out, and sleeps. The Wall Street Journal traveler with the smart attaché case looks right, looks left – is there anybody who will make his day? Careers have begun in the air! With the stewardess he plays the balancing act between grumpy curtness and leery looks at her flanks. He eats the veggies and leaves the dessert, drinks wine ("Do you have a good Pinot Grigio?" "Sorry, sir, we have only Chardonnay.") and feels accomplished but a little tipsy.

The novice traveler drinks only orange juice, but finishes his chicken, including the peas and the dry roll and the pudding. He pulls out his laptop and tries to read his market briefs and study his client's spreadsheets. But the baby drools, the students laugh, and now the fat man in front of him leans back his seat all the way onto the novice' knees. He takes a sleeping pill, puts on the new *Somnus* black eye mask, and leans on his inflatable pillow. But he can't sleep.

Some short business trips are still performed by car. Salesman Willy Loman drove a 1949 Studebaker Champion Business Coupe. John Madden traveled from job to job in a 45-foot bus that has been described as a rolling command post, with high-speed Internet access, multiple TVs, a GPS, cell phones and fax machines – a movable studio in satellite contact with the outside world. The modern Business Trip is, however, an affair of the air. That's also where your trip is being ranked: what you fly and where. As long as you board only a Piper Aztec or Beechcraft Model 18 or fly Horizon Air from Santa Rosa to Los Angeles, you are a Business Trip Apprentice. Regular cross country flights from LA to Dallas on American Airlines earn you the Business Trip Pro label. Four or more international flights per year means you have graduated to the Business Trip Masters level. And when you fly in the company's $18.3 Million Learjet 60XR, you have finally arrived in the elite Business Trip VIP class.

Business Casual

Somewhere between *haute couture* and street grunge lies the fashion terrain of Business Casual. Neglected by GQ and VOGUE and never seen on the catwalks in London, Paris, or Milan, it is nevertheless a look millions of people prepare for every morning when dressing for work. The inattentive observer may only notice Dockers and loafers for men and gender indeterminate pantsuits à la Meg Whitman or Hillary Clinton for women. But such examples don't even begin to express the scope and depth of the term "Business Casual." It has become the label of a thriving new branch of the garment industry, including accessories and hairdos.

A Gallup survey from 2007 found that 34% of men and 52% of women wear Business Casual attire. Only in work environments, where creativity and expertise are less important than status and authority, such as in Congress, in banks, in courts, and at police stations, do the formal suit-and-tie or uniform still reign.

The informal definition of the Business Casual dress code tends to include the abstract requirements of relaxed fit, comfort, neatness, and professionalism (which means, for instance: no piercings). Corporations that *see* themselves as world citizens and *proclaim* environmental consciousness (this includes 98.9% of all publicly traded companies) suggest organically grown fiber dress shirts and closed shoes made from bran. More instructive, however, is a look at current and – alas – past fashion models of Business Casual attire.

Bill Gates of Microsoft: Light-blue flannel shirt (Target brand "Dork") with buttoned-down collar, charcoal-gray dress slacks held up by blue plastic belt, brown shoes from Payless, slightly greasy hair plastered down over part of the forehead by a skillful $7 Supercut coiffeur, faux-gold-rimmed glasses ($30 co-pay), behind which sparkle his eyes with "the angelic clarity characteristic of nearsighted children" (V. Nabokov).

The late great Steve Jobs of Apple and Pixar: Baggy Levi's 501 jeans with thin black leather belt, St. Croix black mock turtleneck sweater with pushed up sleeves (Cashmere and silk), gray 992 New Balance sneakers, rimless granny glasses, 3-day stubble, and short-cropped hairdo somewhere between David Beckham's buzz and Michel Foucault's nothingness.

Carol Bartz formerly of Autodesk and Yahoo: Brightly patterned open blazer, white sleeveless V-neck masculine blouse, with chunky bracelet, black and slightly short slacks (Jones of New York), flat black shoes, size 9, blonde Serengeti lioness hairdo, occasionally potty mouth lipstick.

Martha Stewart of Martha Stewart Living Omnimedia: Medium layered, practical, left-part hairstyle: "To create this style, apply a volumizing product and blow dry using a round brush. Use the round brush to create a little volume in the crown area. Finish off the style by running a flat iron from roots to ends and add shine serum." Add an ankle bracelet, classic Jaclyn Smith pantsuit, high heels, do-it-yourself jewelry: "To transform beads into adornments – necklaces, bracelets, and earrings – you'll send delicate wire through their holes, twisting and looping it so that each stone can be joined to the next."

On casual Fridays, employees are allowed to dress down a notch further from Business Casual. The normally crisp collar of your shirt is allowed to be limp, the shirt cuffs puckered and lumpy, your Dockers wrinkled, and on your feet you may wear non-bran Birkenstocks, with or without socks. You'll see women with their hair in pony-tails, sleeveless tops, and Bermuda shorts. Where's the corporate limit, the borderline where casual turns into a casualty and comfort into comedy – with flip-flops? torn jeans? midriff showing? tattoos? underwear as outerwear?

Because of trespasses of such borderlines, there has been a back-lash to Business Casual, and the fashion pendulum has swung back to well-tailored suits, starched shirts (French cuffs optional), Florsheim dress shoes "polished to a mirror quality spit shine," no fake Rolexes, no ear or nose hair. Speaking of grooming, the look of "New Business Formal" has been admirably expressed in the essay "Professional Dress Code Tips" by Donald K. Burleson: "If you have been working all night and have an early morning meeting, you can use an anti-inflammatory hemorrhoid cream (e.g. Preparation H) to quickly shrink those unsightly puffy bags under your eyes. Just carefully dab the roid cream on your lower eyelids (being careful not to get any in your eyes) and you will look fresh and well-rested."

The Computer

The Computer is, as Wire Magazine puts it, a "pervasive phenomenon" in Corporate America, especially in departments where high productivity is not a major goal. Hence, while the Computer doesn't contribute much to output and profit, it is part of the ambiance like the potted plant and the ergonomic chair, and as such it adds to Corporate Culture.

The computer serves ten main purposes: play games, watch porn, play music, write memos, calculate income taxes using spreadsheets, read and send e-mails, store and print stuff, watch videos, google your own name, and build a facebook page.

To meet these sophisticated needs, cunning manufacturers have built very sophisticated machines. Wonders of silicon ingenuity with many Gigs of memory, they have raised large portions of the American intelligentsia and entire populations of corporate employees to higher levels of literacy. As an example of such progress, consider this: No reader has to go anymore through the awkward ordeal of turning a page of a book by hand! No sir: In order to move from one e-book page to another, you simply use a mouse or, alternatively, the mostly rectangular so-called touchpad in the front middle of your laptop (better clean it first of crumbs). To start the page-turning process, (1) find the arrow on the right side of your window that displays page # n of your book, or (2) click on the screen with page # n in preparation of using the mouse wheel (you should always have a mouse with a wheel!), and then (3) scroll (not turn!) the screen by either (a) moving the aforementioned arrow in the desired direction, or (b) operate the wheel with a finger (middle or forefinger) in the desired direction, or (c) slide one of your fingers on the aforementioned touchpad while also possibly (it depends) using the buttons in front of said touchpad – and voilà, you'll get page # n+1 in no time! A very similar and quite easy to memorize procedure applies when you want to go from page # n back to the previous page # n-1.

Speaking of progress, the famed computerologist Professor Berthold Bummelböhm compares the advance from the ancient slide-rule to the modern computer with the advance from the piano to the player piano. "A computer," he reminds us, "will not expand our innate human attributes such as creativity and imagination, nor will it improve our most valuable primitive impulses of fight, fear, fight, and fornication. Rather, like the player piano or its spiritual twin, the television set, it gives you more limited, and therefore more rational, choices. With one or two mouse-clicks," - here the professor takes some time to demonstrate – "you can download an audio file from which a pleasant voice nicely summarizes Melville's *Moby Dick* in four minutes, and equally fast you will find a dozen different YouTube performances of Beethoven's piano concerto No. 5 in E-flat major, Op. 73. Compare this to the agony of reading 470 pages of Melville's prose or having to use many of the 88 piano keys yourself!"

Furthermore, politicians and CEOs of computer manufacturers have rightfully pointed out that the Computer has created tens of millions of jobs, second only to the number of useless jobs it has abolished. A book, Bummelböhm points out, originally produced by the printing press à la Gutenberg, can now be reprinted by means of a computer. Since the computer has, after sluggish beginnings, emphasized colors and pictures over letters and sentences, the human mind and its wetware brain have adjusted accordingly and finally achieved what color TV originally set out to accomplish: the development of our prefrontal lobe, which blocks out nonsense and fosters doubt, critical thinking, and self-awareness, has been halted and reversed in favor of redecorating efforts geared at both the occipital cortex and the parietal cortex. These are the older evolutionary segments in the back of our brains, where pictures of the visual world are processed together with all sorts of entertainment features. Magnetic imaging shows both these primitive cortices are highly active in the brains of infants, chimpanzees, and children up to age five, and they also light up in adults who are engrossed in looking at a computer screen or watching a movie on TV (at the same time, the prefrontal lobe goes dormant).

Yes, Bummelböhm concludes, one still hears the occasional Luddite criticism of the Computer; but one should give such negativism neither space no credence. In the long run, people will no doubt become more and more Computer-friendly, cherishing their laptops and iPads and smartphones like pets or kids. And computers, in turn, will become much more people-literate, figure us out ever more, and manipulate us – just as our pets and kids do.

E-Mail

Imagine a carefree college grad Bert in a new job as an associate engineer at a large firm (let's call it Augur, Inc.) being blamed by his manager X for a mistake he didn't make (yes, that does happen). Miffed, Bert returns to his cubicle and writes an email calling his manager X a jerk to his friend Ernie who works at another company. Ernie emails back and suggests that Bert quit Augur and join his company. Now imagine that April in the cubicle next to Bert's is an ear-witness to the scene when manager X balls out Bert. While Bert is sending his e-mail, April is texting her friend May a few choice words about manager X (who considers himself quite a Lothario). She texts about his office dalliances and uses the expression "scum bag". May works as a police officer in a SWAT team. She's tough, had worked at a vice squad and is well versed in the sex-drenched vernacular of pimps and prostitutes. Via her pager, she sends a text message back to April, calling manager X a prick, and worse, adding ironically that Augur, Inc. must be very proud of manager X.

It feels so good to vent over e-mail! It's private, it's free speech, and it's not only password-protected but shielded by the Fourth Amendment ("The right of the people to be secure in their persons, houses, papers, and effects, against unreasonable searches and seizures, shall not be violated ..."). Or is it? No, it isn't.

The reality is this. Augur, Inc. owns its e-mail system. This fact is reason enough to allow Augur to review the content of Bert's message to Ernie, as well as Ernie's reply to Bert, even though his was sent from another company. The same holds true for April's text message and May's pager message. May, a public employee, would fall under a ruling known as *City of Ontario v. Quon*. This case went all the way to the Supreme Court, which unanimously upheld the warrentless search of a police officer's personal messages on a government-owned pager. The background: The city of Ontario had obtained a transcript of officer Quon's messages, some of them sexually explicit, during an investigation to determine whether officers were using their pagers for personal messages and exceeded their character limits on text messages. The reason for this investigation was the city's concern whether it needed to modify its wireless contract, which imposed extra fees when employees exceeded their limits. Bottom line: There was no violation of officer Quon's constitutional Fourth Amendment rights, because the search was motivated by reasonable work-related purposes. That's how the Supreme Court ruled.

But that's not all. Even if you are using your private e-mail (not government or company-owned), including web mail such as yahoo mail or Google's gmail, you can't expect privacy. If Bert shows April the personal e-mail message he sent to Ernie, for instance by forwarding it, he will lose his Fourth Amendment protections of privacy. The Supreme Court "consistently has held that a person has no legitimate expectation of privacy in information he voluntarily turns over to third parties." *Smith v. Maryland*, 442 U.S. 735, 743-44, 99 S. Ct. 2577, 2582 (1979).

CEOs also send e-mails, and as the top representative of a company they always set an example of clean, polite, and informative messages. Following is an example.

In an article in the online edition of FORTUNE magazine, writer Philip Elmer-DeWitt had posted a mildly critical and rather gossipy article about the resignation of Mark Hurd as CEO of Hewlett Packard. In it he quoted from a Washington Post profile of Larry Ellison, Oracle's CEO, who is widely known as the "Lothario of the pocket-protector set in Silicon Valley." Ellison hasn't denied having had liaisons with some of his attractive employees, even had to face a sexual harassment suit filed by one Adelyn Lee. Hurd paid off his consort Jodie and no suit ensued, while – as Elmer-Dewitt duly noted – Ellison's one-time lover Adelyn "enhanced" some e-mails to make Ellison look guilty, and for this infraction she was convicted. Still, a peeved Ellison rushed to the keyboard to send just such a clean, polite, and informative message. His e-mail reads as follows:

From: Larry Ellison
Subject: *Hey Jerk*
Date: August 11, 2010 1:00:55 PM EDT
To: PHILIP ELMER-DEWITT

Adelyn Lee went to jail for a year for falsely accusing me of sexual harassment. Why did you leave that out of your story you scum bag? Let me guess ... your job is telling half-truths. Fortune Magazine must be very proud of you.

Rightsizing

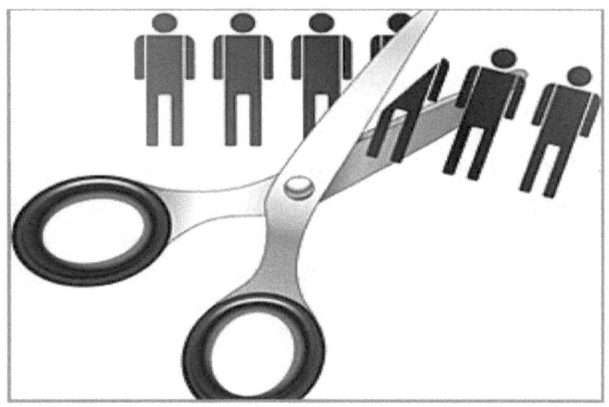

Adam and Eve were not only the first human beings (at least according to the Old Testament) and the first customers (of the snake), they were also the first two people dismissed from the (easy) job they were doing at the time: walking around naked while testing fruit growing in paradise.

This story in Genesis is a rather extreme example of reducing a workforce – downsizing a team of two to zero. Corporations prefer the word *rightsizing* over *downsizing* or *dismissing* people. Luther's bible has God use the phrase "showing Adam the exit" and "expelling" him. Like any manager in charge, God punished Adam and Eve's disobedience by laying them off. But in addition he made sure that his "Enterprise Paradise" be closed to humans forever. To this end he has, to this day, the entrances watched and guarded by security personnel, the so called Cherubim. As far as we know (sources are scant and unreliable) the snake, temptress and instigator of Adam and Eve's transgression, was physically harmed by God clipping its legs, but was allowed to live on in paradise, though severely disabled.

The version of history of mankind, in which man is viewed as a working and supervised animal, should be told – not as a class struggle but – as a story of the struggle between rightsizing by the mighty and, when told from the opposing camp of the powerlessly employed, as a story of trying to avoid being sacked, canned, axed, fired, terminated.

Here is space for only a few examples of rightsizing and, on the other hand, of keeping a job against severe odds. Continuing with God: He is on record for several more dramatic dismissals. For instance, when he forced out Lucifer and sent him to hell. This firing was very consequential: it made God and Lucifer into adversaries, with both of them fighting about man's soul ever since. Had God kept Lucifer on his staff, by retraining and giving him some adequate celestial responsibilities, we might have a different world today.

Zeus, to mention another boss, had a staff where each of his reporting gods had a well-defined portfolio and responsibility. Hephaistos was in charge of fire and weapons, Athena owned art and science, Hermes was in charge of the mail system and of thieves, and so on. Compared to Jesus and his staff who wandered all over creation, Zeus had a headquarters, the Olympus, where everybody had their office. It was here at the Olympus that Hephaistos once took Hera's side against Zeus, who promptly fired him - threw him out with such force that from that day on Hephaistos had a bad limp. They made up later and Hephaistos was rehired, in part because he was a great architect and built palaces for Zeus and his staff. Zeus did not make the Lucifer mistake. Instead, he and his brothers Hades and Poseidon divided up the world into three separate markets, the heavens, hell, and the oceans, without interfering with each other.

In the episode of Noah and his ark, God acted even more rash and vindictive, like a manager who is frustrated and under stress. His rightsizing (the big flood) was very original, but also elaborate and cruel. At the last moment before the deluge he let Noah choose a team of survivors and got rid of all remaining living creatures by drowning them.

Jesus, God's son and junior executive, hired twelve department managers, his disciples or, in the original Greek, the *mathetai* (plural, the singular disciple is *mathetes*). They were the learners and followers, the next generation trained to sell and implement Jesus' teachings. Although Jesus had favorites and was critical of others, he dismissed only one of the twelve, Judas Iscariot, the treasurer of Jesus' company. Judas had acted like a whistle blower for the Roman high priests and betrayed Jesus by distorting his objectives and identifying him to the soldiers (by the "Judas kiss"). When Jesus let him go, it was too late, the harm was already done.

Adam, already downsized by God, should in turn have laid off a troublemaker from his farm east of Eden, his very own son Cain, before he murdered Abel. Sometimes family bonds, lenience, or nepotism hinder the necessary rightsizing. Caesar, too, was naive, trusting his colleague and friend Brutus, whose firing from the senate he could have easily effected, but didn't, to his detriment, as is well known from the events on the Ides of March.

There exist countless other examples where retaining a person rather than firing him would have changed history. Take, for instance, Galilei, who was, after several warnings since 1616, finally fired 1633 by his former friend, Pope Urban VIII, who had felt insulted by (allegedly) being depicted as a simpleton (the figure Simplicio in Galilei's *Dialogue Concerning the Two Chief World Systems*). If Urban hadn't been so miffed, Galilei could have continued his research under papal protection, and modern science would possibly have flourished earlier and from within the catholic church, who knows? And what about Hillary Clinton, who was fired by the Electoral College even before she could be hired?

Information

Karl Marx believed that the history of mankind must be described as the history of class struggles, as a battle of economic dominance against the powerless worker, who will, miraculously, win in the end. Today even Marxists concede that talk about different classes has been replaced by chatter about different standards of living, and the historic class struggle has turned into an histrionic scuffle about the power of information and who owns and dominates it, leading to the kerfuffle over the claim that Information (not knowledge) is power.

In politics and large corporations, the equation Information = Power has been accompanied by the more aggressive battle cry "Power beats Knowledge." The background: Enlightened corporate philosophers have realized that the alleged evolution from Information to Knowledge, and Power via Knowledge, is an historic misunderstanding that must be replaced by its opposite, by reading it from right to left: Power creates facts and thus Knowledge, which in turn is distributed as Information. Therefore, Information is the source, the cause and axiom of corporate Power. Knowledge is a byproduct, not more than a footnote, subject to the main text of facts and factoids, news and opinions created by this Power. The ownership of Information has replaced the ownership of the old means of material production.

Marx knew this in 1845:. He wrote: "The class which has the means of material production at its disposal, has control at the same time over the means of mental production, so that thereby, generally speaking, the ideas of those who lack the means of mental production are subject to it." (From *German Ideology*).

The emerging power broker in this historic advance is the CIO, the Chief Information Officer. He is the new Scrooge, not wading in gold coins but in data, the raw material of Information. Twenty years ago, he was proud to manage 365,000,000 pages of computer printout (so-called hard copies) a year for the average American corporation. Most of these, 349,000,000 to be exact, are never read, and so the CIO had to find new media to send, route, store, and destroy the same information all over again. Nowadays, the CIO's amount of data has been multiplied by a hundred thousand, which is irrelevant in practical terms, because still nobody reads this stockpile of raw information. Yet in terms of Power the huge amount is relevant: just like a stockpile of nuclear weapons, Information and Data intimidate and maintain a subtle balance between competing corporations, which all own, give or take, the same data and the same Information.

Internal to a corporation, sensitive and confidential Information flows through the electronic channels under the heading of EI, Executive Information. Middle managers are supplied by the traditional MIS, the Management Information System, and the Yahoo Unknown Corporate Citizen (YUCC) feeds off the samizdat nipples of underground Unix notes and proletarian email.

Information and its even more potent bastard siblings, misinformation and disinformation, are composed of data. However, only a small portion of all data is tangible and dependent upon facts. Another, larger, part is meaningless propaganda about benefits, reorganizations and the (better) future of the Corporation. By far the majority of corporate Information represents what linguists call Speech Acts. This is a language-based activity with a specific intention to influence opinions or to tamper with the course of things without stating, or denying, a single fact. Rather, the creator of the Speech Act has the deliberate purpose of bringing about, through sentences, a calculated effect. Take, for instance, the CEO's message urging employees to disregard certain misinformation about layoffs. His implicit intent is to discredit contradictory Information, thus showing that most Information is about some other Information. Such a layered approach protects the so-called Information Worker from the hard knocks of reality.

Sub-classes of Information are Gossip and Rumor, including the confidential Rumor, which has the highest speed of spreading - largely due to another corporate character, the Computer.

Marketing & Advertising

They are like Tweedledee and Tweedledum, the twins from Lewis Carroll's book *Through the Looking-Glass and What Alice Found There*:

> Tweedledum and Tweedledee
> Agreed to have a battle;
> For Tweedledum said Tweedledee
> Had spoiled his nice new rattle.

From this nursery rhyme it is clear that Tweedledee acts in the role of a Marketing guy spoiling the nice new rattle, which is, of course, a metaphor for the noisy ad campaign put out by the Advertising guy, alias Tweedledum. Usually, however, Tweedledum and Tweedledee don't only look and act alike; they finish each other's sentences.

We know (from the chapter on *The Customer*) that Adam and Eve were the first customers in biblical times, and the snake was the first salesperson. The fruit on the forbidden tree in paradise was the first advertised product. It was God himself, playing the first Tweedledum, who did the Advertising. Pointing out that by eating the fruit from the tree of knowledge Adam and Eve would know good and evil, God was promoting the forbidden fruit. That's what Advertising does: issuing an enticing ad intended to persuade a customer to pay a certain price for a desired product, where the ad includes the name, the price, the location of the product, and how that product would benefit the consumer, Adam and Eve in this case. Especially by highlighting the benefit, knowing good and evil, God made the product very attractive, and this closed the sale, which was easily executed by the snake, albeit at a high price for the customers Adam and Eve: expulsion from paradise.

In the traditional theory of the Marketing-Mix, Advertising was still called Promotion. The mix consisted of the so-called 4 P's: Promotion, Product, Price, Place (where the sale takes place; think location, location, location, for instance Paradise). Promotion and Advertising became necessary, when the actual *need* for products diminished and the salesmen had to cater to *wants* – which had to be stimulated. Advertising gained in importance even more, when the 4 P's made room for a more customer-centric model. First, the Product became a "Solution;" Promotion was elevated to second rank and called "Information;" third, Price was upgraded to "Value," which makes buying and spending money almost a moral obligation; and finally, fourth, Place was broadened to "Access" – via all kinds of distribution channels, including the Internet. The supply-side 4 P's model had become the demand-side SIVA model: Solution, Information, Value, Access.

More recently, Advertising has begun to dominate Marketing, sometimes replaced it outright. Three interrelated developments have contributed to this change: (1) involvement of the customer, (2) new media and new technologies, and (3) cheating.

Regarding point (1) - involvement of the customer: It is obvious that customers have become voluntary carriers of brand advertising, wearing shirts and shoes with company logos prominently displayed on them. To deepen the involvement, crowd-sourcing has become a fad on TV and the Internet, where consumers are cajoled into creating the ads by which they will later be swayed to buy what they themselves have advertised. Examples are the Doritos commercial in recent Super Bowl broadcasts. Other companies such as Google, Nike, Hershey's and General Mills have launched contests that have created enthusiastic consumer engagement and media buzz, and a surge of herd behavior, which makes for great advertising copy as well (crowded restaurants must have good food!).

Regarding point (2) - new media and new technologies: Tablets, smartphones and many other portable digital devices have Internet access, and through this route we expose ourselves to a brave new world of social networking, where advertising sneaks into web mail, web searches, banner ads, pop-ups, pop-unders, flash, blogs, online newspapers, private websites, and every search engine page. An especially compelling new trend is the niche advertising concept based on the so-called "Long Tail" theory – selling a large number of unique items in relatively small quantities, in other words, selling less of more, as Amazon, Netflix. iTunes, and Google do. (See Chris Anderson's book *The Long Tail: Why the Future of Business Is Selling Less of More*.)

Finally, regarding point (3) - cheating: The resource pool of unethical Marketing and Advertising increases daily, not only through the old-fashioned techniques of email spam, adware, and borderline lies like puffery. A newer advance here is the so-called shill. A shill receives money or other rewards for pretending to be a satisfied customer who gives glowing testimonials to the merits of a product or service. Examples are fake book reviews at the Amazon online book store, positive restaurant reviews submitted to yelp.com by employees and owners of the reviewed restaurant (which is also called astroturfing, an ironic name for fake grass-root customer responses).

Marketing and Advertising have come a long way since causing the fall from grace in paradise. But perhaps they've always been essentially the same. Doesn't it seem that God, as early as the time of Genesis, already cheated Adam and Eve, with the snake as a shill?

The Memo

What is a Memo? The short answer is: one page, one topic, one author. It is the smallest unit of official inner-company communication from person A to several persons B, C, D, … etc. In many cases it is still conservatively printed on white paper, or sent by email. In most cases it is the longest literary document ever written by A, and the longest ever read by B, C, D, … etc.

A memo must not contain more than one subject matter, express one single thought, and pursue one specific purpose. In this sense it resembles a tweet or a 15 second TV commercial; they all require the same attention span. But different from a tweet and a commercial, a memo must be careful with the truth, because occasionally it may be taken seriously. "Do not pass along untrue reports," is the warning word of Exodus 23:1. Many a memo is written purely for a particular informational purpose: "Management is happy to inform you that the company contribution for your 401(k) has been reduced from 5% to 2%. Best regards, Management." Others contain an urgent request laced with so-called action items: "Management is happy to introduce the new *Sales Information Log and LibrarY* (henceforward referred to by the acronym *SILLY*). As a state-of-the-art web-based system, it will require you to perform 18 procedural steps instead of the 6 steps in the old PC-based system and thus save time and money. In a first phase, you are required to … (and so it goes on for one entire page). Best regards, Management."

In addition to these old-fashioned memos, a new type of memo has appeared, a hybrid of high-strung memorandum and spam email. It is the flaming memo, or "flame" for short. The name suggests a blazing, passionate burst of verbal energy unleashed in well-ordered bits and bytes over electronic channels. Hidden in the safety, but not quite the anonymity, of his rectangular cubicle, the flame thrower composes brilliant flashes about his own deep resentments, or else his highfalutin ideas to influence the course of his corporation's history. Since a fair amount of unbridled passion is involved, a flame often releases more heat from the heart than cool from the cortex. But once the bytes are out and on the wire, the red-hot feelings will be public knowledge, all too often finding an ice-cold reception at the other end. Compare the effect of such a temperamental flare with an ardent love letter written by candlelight around midnight, after which it will lose the letter writer's dithyrambic fire in the transmission over the wire and appear the next morning before your lover's eyes as the eccentric ramblings of a lovelorn fool.

A disrespected but popular form of the flaming memo is the nasty-gram. This flame contains either some spiteful personal criticism or pent-up anger directed at the Corporate World, cc-ed to co-workers. As the Old Testament says, "And my anger shall flame out against you" (Exodus 22:24). Most of these personal memoranda are self-righteous or self-pitying, and generally do nothing for the career of their author.

It is important to mention also the "leaked memo," an internal, usually confidential memorandum sent to a limited distribution of trusted insiders, one of whom decides that the memo should be known more widely. He forwards it to the press or posts it anonymously on the web. Such amateur whistle-blowers can be fired immediately if found out (remember that company email is not private!). At the same time, a company spokesperson will say that (1), the published memo is not authentic but simply a rumor, and (2), even if the memo is authentic, the company will make no comment, and (3), "We never comment on any of those reports in The Inquirer," so spoke former HP spokesman Ryan Donovan, "because we don't consider them true media, but more of a rumor sheet." The latter announcement was made when the British online tech journal *The Inquirer* had quoted from an in-house memo that HP was hoping to improve profits by laying off 14,500 American workers and replacing them with cheaper labor from Guadalajara, Costa Rica, and Bangalore.

A Google search for "leaked"and "confidential memo" brought up 67,000 hits, from Walmart, Microsoft, Oracle, CNN, the Tobacco Institute, the White House, and several government agencies such as the CIA. There exists now a central place where at least the most blatant memo leaks are being collected and systematically made public, at wikileaks.org.

A brilliant memo, a concise and constructive presidential tweet, was written by Abraham Lincoln on July 18, 1863, to the War Department, regarding a court martialed deserter:

"Let him fight instead of being shot."

The Org Chart

The Org Chart is the corporate version of a hierarchy, a word that originally indicated the rule and power of a high priest and then came to mean the rank order of angels. This celestial analogy helps us understand the top-down pecking order that is today's Org Chart.

According to the first letter of Peter (1 Peter 3:22), as recorded in the New Testament, Jesus Christ, after ascending to heaven, took control of the flock of angels, which made him, in a manner of speaking, the new CEO of the entire organization, while God took a more strategic back office role as Chairman of the Board. With certain variations and deviations here and there, the hierarchy of angels – also called the Choir of Angels – has, since the middle ages, been a stable affair of three spheres, each one with three layers. The first sphere is made up of the top angels called Seraphim, Cherubim, and Ophanim. Seraphim are very close to the office where Jesus works, and since their main duty is a continuous shout of "holy, holy, holy," they closely resemble executive vice presidents. Cherubim and Ophanim are more operational, guarding with their swords the Garden of Eden and the heavenly Budget Ledger, the way senior VPs and ordinary VPs protect their respective divisional turfs of Sales, Marketing, R&D, Operations, IT, and so on. One step down from the top angels, angels of the second sphere correspond roughly to functional managers, directors, and other middle managers. Finally, the third sphere consists of Ruler Angels, Archangels, and Guardian Angels. Only these latter three characters work directly with ordinary employees, just as department managers, managers, and supervisors must get close to their "reports." There exists a fierce competition at this lowest level of management, because it is, perhaps paradoxically, from here that the higher-ups, the Cherubim and Ophanim in their role as Vice Presidents, choose the next generation of corporate leaders, while middle managers of the second sphere usually stay put. Here, at the management level of plain angels and archangels, the crucial distinctions become visible: Which angel/manager is just a Hands-On, who is already a Has-Been, and which department manager is, like the archangel Michael, a Fair-Haired Boy who, looking already like a cherub, will rise fast with a chance of becoming a Seraph?

The Bible is full of Org-Charts. Depicted in da Vinci's painting "The Last Supper" we see a "flat" Org Chart consisting only of Jesus and the twelve disciples reporting to him, including Judas, fourth from the left, elbow on the table and ready to be fired. Or take Moses and his second-in-command Joshua, plus his PR man Aaron, Moses' brother. A deeper Org Chart is given in the apocryphal Book of Judith. At the top of it stands proudly King Nebuchadnezzar of Assyria. Reporting to him is his "commander-in-chief Holofernes, who was second only to himself." Below Holofernes are the marshals, then the generals, and finally the corps of officers. Further down the branches follow "as the King had commanded, a hundred and twenty thousand infantry and twelve thousand mounted archers, all picked men." To these report, in turn, "an immense number of camels, donkeys, and mules for the baggage, innumerable sheep, oxen, and goats for provisions." Also mentioned are nobles and the eunuch Bagoas. However, eunuchs and nobles play no active role in the fighting and were probably employed only in certain staff functions like Quality Control and HR.

As the example of Nebuchadnezzar's organization shows, an Org Chart can be divided, from top to bottom, into (1) overhead (i.e., executive management), (2) middle managers, and (3) professionals. In recent years, overhead and professionals have squeezed the middle layer and flattened out Org Charts, at the expense of making them grow broader and fatter to the left and right. This is the law of the conservation of managers. Here's why: First, you will percolate up the chart (like hot water in an espresso machine) and become a manager, if you produce enough heat and there's a vacuum above you. By contrast, the free fall from managerial grace like

Lucifer's tumble from heaven is rare. Companies don't want fallen semi-gods mingle with true professionals, because they may tell them how mortal the immortals at the top really are. So, instead, these fallen angels become strategic advisors on special assignments, like the Corporate Gentleman treated elsewhere in this collection, creating their own branches and twigs to the side of the trunk of the corporate tree, where there's more shade than sun and where they wait for their golden parachute and have important meetings with all the other noble Bagoasses.

Important as Org Charts are in post-biblical times, there is one event that turns an Org Chart from a status-quo document into a volatile instrument for the interpretation of corporate politics. The event is, of course, the internal reorganization of people, power, and positions, the Re-Org. A good Re-Org fuels the dynamics that moves a company from one relatively unstable state into another unstable state. The new Org Chart becomes the updated Hierarchy of Angels, and so it goes on forever.

Powerpoint

Powerpoint (or PowerPoint, sometimes affectionately abbreviated as PPT) is, as everyone has known since his days in kindergarten, Microsoft's program for graphs, charts, and bullet pointed presentations. Although you can add clip art, moving objects ("Fly in From Right") and jingles, all of which illustrate its motto of "style over substance," it has stolidly preserved its status as the tool of choice for corporate group-think. Powerpoint slides create the illusion that we understand a problem, no matter how complex, because it looks much simpler with bullet points. Viewers in the audience are usually so thoroughly enthralled that they have been described as looking like "hypnotized chickens."

As the facilitator of group-think, Powerpoint is pervasive in the military, popular in corporate meetings, and loved as a convenient substitute for lengthy textbooks and those time-consuming lectures at universities.

In the military: During the run-up to the invasion of Iraq, General Tommy Franks gave the enemy a fair chance to mobilize and catch up because his PPT strategy took so much time. Instead of explicit, written orders, he passed out elaborate Powerpoint slides, which caused puzzlement and frustration, because his men were often baffled as to the proper interpretation of the bullet points (see Thomas Ricks' book *Fiasco: The American Military in Iraq*). Ever since, among officers, bullet points go under the name of "friendly Microsoft fire."

Turn to civilian life: Al Gore won an Academy Award and a Nobel Prize with a nicely done Powerpoint presentation. And who can forget Ross Perot's slides during the presidential campaign 1992, which won him the hearts and minds of many television viewers and 18.9% of the popular vote – 19,743,821 liked him and his slides (8.4% still voted for him in 1996). Perot's fondness for graphs and charts was handsomely displayed on his website PerotCharts.com, now redirecting you to Ron Paul's Liberty Forest.

Academia: Lest we chalk up PPT-philia only to the geekiness of politicians and eccentrics, let me remind you that Paul Krugman, professor and liberal Op-Ed blogger, gave his 2008 prize lecture for the Nobel Prize in Economics as a slide presentation: check the Nobel Prize website where it is reproduced in pdf format. Be aware that especially at universities the dominance of PPT is threatened by better alternatives from Apple and cheaper alternatives from Apache's Open Office.

A first-rate PPT presentation may win you, too, an Oscar, a Nobel, or votes. But what is first-rate? Here are eleven proven rules, in bullet format for easy comprehension:

- One thought (idea, concept) per slide

- Colors: Blue and Black for management; add Red for Sales; never use Yellow, Pink, or Teal

- Style: Declarative sentences: think the book *Dick and Jane*

- Start with a quote by your CEO, end with a *Dilbert* cartoon (use *The Far Side* or other more sophisticated cartoons at your own risk and only when you know your audience well)

- When presenting to R&D, insert a slide mocking Marketing

- When presenting to Marketing, insert a slide mocking R&D

- The first half of your presentation should tell a story

- The second half should show numbers that corroborate your story

- Number your slides in the format "page 17 of 89" so that the audience knows how long to look like hypnotized chickens

- Make a joke every 7th slide (there exist PPT slide joke books)

- Make eye contact with alpha dogs in the audience

In order to counter the image of Powerpoint as the most awkward and boring communication tool in the world, good only for the likes of Doofus Drake, Microsoft has launched a secret project, not in their engineering division, but in the Entertainment division. In support of this effort, Microsoft's Xbox content engineers have begun creating PPT versions of the Bible, the Odyssey, the Genji monogatari, Hamlet, and The Bridges of Madison County. This is not an easy endeavor. For instance, regarding The Bridges with Meryl Streep and Clint Eastwood, several blogs have leaked that Xbox engineers were easily able to code Eastwood's sudden appearance (they used "Fly in From Right" animation) but are still unsure about how to best render Meryl's choice remark to Clint, "I was just going to have some iced tea and split the atom, but that can wait."

The Staff Meeting

Staff meetings are the bane of staff members, but not for the staff's manager. One would think that spending an hour with your peers and away from your cubicle will refresh you, or at least let you goof off without email or demanding customers. Far from it. All employees, except the manager (who is often less computer-literate), carry their laptops, tablets, smart phones into the meeting room, pretending to have all necessary data at their fingertips, but of course mainly reading and writing emails, sending texts, checking their Facebook and twitter accounts, and skimming through news and baseball scores while the manager conducts the meeting.

The word "conducts" hints at an almost symphonic complexity. In spite of the continuous electronic distractions mentioned above, a manager knows that a meeting needs to be "structured" into several movements in order to have a purpose stated at the beginning, a process in the middle, and a result at the end. At the risk of boring the experienced employee who has probably sat through more staff meetings than through church services, here is, for the corporate neophyte, a quick synopsis of what to expect.

First movement: There must be an opening theme, normally called an "agenda", put together by the manager. The agenda lists the topics the way a symphonic overture does: in bullet form, hinted, not fully spelled out. The Latin word "agenda" is a so called gerundivum, indicating, by way of the ending n-d-a, that the topics (plural) "need to be" acted upon in the present meeting or afterwards. Fifth and last movement: a protocol of the meeting, called "minutes", written up usually by a dedicated, or appointed, employee. In it, details (minutiae) of the discussion, progress reports, so called "action items", open problems are recorded for posterity and for the next staff meeting, when the minutes are "read and approved".

The middle movements 2, 3, and 4 develop, as was the case for classical composers from Haydn to Beethoven, the theme of the meeting, elaborate the various topics and leitmotifs the staff members are working on in their cubicles. The second movement may thus treat the most urgent item in a serious, *allegro con brio* voice: project delays, customer complaints, new managerial directives, and the like. The third movement tends to be more cheerful, conducted in a dancing mode, *allegro vivace ma non troppo*, where employees report on their progress. So called "next steps", small corrections, suggestions for the future, action items, and possibly rehashes ("coda": "let me repeat what I said before ...") are presented in the fourth movement, often in *andante* or *allegro molto*.

Just as the relaxing hour you spend in a pub after a concert that you *had to* attend without really *wanting to*, staff members will not return immediately to their cubicles, but convene at the Water Cooler to exchange some comments on coworkers or management. Or they conduct a more informal post-meeting meeting in the cafeteria, needing a more comforting desserts than on other days.

The manager meanwhile leaves his staff by peeling off to the side like a believer who has just spent too much time with agnostics and atheists. His work done for the week, he disappears into his cubicle, a priest joining up with the Corporate Spirit.

The Self-Evaluation

In order to help current and future corporate citizens achieve success, the following form for an employee's self-evaluation is offered here as a tool for self-reflection. Notice, however, that "reflection" is not a corporate term, it never appears in a company's Employee Handbook. Therefore, one should not confuse that what the company is looking for in a self-evaluation with an invitation to ponder one's self-worth.

Sometimes an employee is, in addition, asked to rate himself / herself, using grades like "Far below level,", "Below level", "At level", "Above level", "Far exceeding level." Or give yourself the mark F, D, C, B, or A. Or points from one to five. Scales like these have been popularized by corporations like Amazon, which asks customers to rate their products on a similar rating scale. Once an employee has filled out his so-called Self-Eval form, it is forwarded to the employee's manager. This manager will then pitch his own assessment against the self-evaluation of his employee. If discrepancies arise, the employee's grade is discarded and replaced by the manager's.

A Self-Eval form will likely contain the following categories (with explanations for the employee):

PROFESSIONAL ACHIEVEMENTS

Describe your most significant professional accomplishment(s) during the review period. As to each, comment on the challenges you faced and how you met those challenges.

Note: Discuss how well you think you have done in achieving the goals you set for yourself last year and how you have developed and matured as a corporate citizen. To the extent you fell short of your goals, please indicate what may have caused that to happen.

PROFESSIONAL ABILITIES

With respect to your professional abilities, discuss your three main strengths and up to three areas where you think you need to develop or improve. Consider research skills, analytical skills, written expression, oral expression, judgment, and substantive knowledge and breadth of experience in your area of expertise.

VALUE ADDED

Productivity/Efficiency. If you fell substantially short of the performance measures given to you by management after your last evaluation (sales quota, lines of code, marketing campaigns, software updates installed, etc.), please state the reason(s) for the shortfall.

PERSONAL QUALITIES

With respect to your personal qualities, discuss your three main strengths and up to three areas where you think you need to develop or improve. Per the evaluation criteria, consider: internal and external interaction, flexibility, willingness to take on extra work, leadership, personal attitudes, interest in and loyalty to the Corporation.

OBJECTIVES FOR THE NEXT REVIEW PERIOD

Outline your professional objectives for the next 12 months, including: (a) the type of work you wish to handle and the type of work experiences or opportunities you wish to be assigned; (b) the professional skills and personal qualities you wish to acquire or improve upon, and your plans for doing so; (c) if you are a 3rd year (or more) senior staff member in your department, state the further career development you plan to pursue or become involved with, either individually or as part of a team.

One of the corporate benefits of such a form consists in making the employee feel small like a child again, trying with downcast eyes to justify bad behavior in front of a stern parent or school principal.

Notice that since the 1980s the automatic increase algorithm of your salary (based on seniority, experience, degrees, loyalty to the company) has been replaced by a simpler and therefore more just system, taking into account only your value for the company. As the value of a company's stock can go up and down, so may also your value for the company. Remember that you are giving your expertise to the company, which employs and pays you for that gift. If the value of your expertise diminishes by becoming obsolete, or by being offered cheaper by a younger employee, the amount of your salary will naturally go down. This new algorithm is called "merit system." Salary increases will be done strictly as "merit increases". Merit increases may be negative or positive. Please make a note of it.

Wall Street and its Journal

On Wall Street fortunes are lost and won, but never earned.

For many people, Wall Street is easy to understand and hard to like, and the same goes for its Journal, the WSJ. Both Wall Street and its Journal are religiously simple-minded with a clear-cut morality, despite an abundance of polysyllabic words with which the WSJ describes and justifies the machinations of Wall Street. Simple-minded religion and clear-cut morality? Yes, because its axioms are straightforward Operational Perversions of the Ten Commandments:

1. Mammon is your God, and that's that

2. As your idol, you may choose gold, bonds, stocks, or any other security

3. It is vain to talk about Mammon; shut up and make money

4. Remember that the Stock Market stays closed on Sabbath, Sundays, and holidays

5. Honor your parents; but better for them is a good assisted-care home

6. If you can, make a kill

7. Adultery is not a leading indicator of business failure

8. Thou shalt not steal outright

9. If you get an excellent stock tip, keep it to yourself

10. Since stock trading is a zero-sum game (your gain has to be paid for by your neighbor's loss) you need to covet and eventually take what belongs to your neighbor

These Operational Perversions have an impact on your life. In a nutshell: Whatever is good for you and your neighbor is bad for

Wall Street. And what is good for Wall Street is usually bad for you and your neighbor.

For instance, when you and your neighbor, and their neighbors too, are laid off, Wall Street and its Journal will rejoice about how the savings improve the bottom line, and that the stock price of your (former) company will rise. No wonder that the WSJ will describe an increase of minimum wage as disastrous for the economy, and any such analysis is supported by an allegedly convincing graph. If food prices go up due to droughts or disasters, then that's bad for you but good for Wall Street, because lower supply raises prices and profits, and the Journal is again happy. If, however, your company decides to reduce prices for a product so that you and your neighbors can afford it, or if the Board of Directors approves a high dividend payment, then the company's stock will drop and the Journal will question the wisdom of the Board and describe the future of your company in the gloomiest terms. It is that easy. If Wall Street is happy, you won't be; if you have reasons to celebrate, Wall Street will find reasons to warn of the decline of Western civilization. When you are happy and at peace, Wall Street panics. The WSJ is succinct: "Peace is bearish."

Often agreeing with pundits from low-brow Fox News, but with more college degrees, the Wall Street Journal has always had its pet theories, such as the ancient gold standard (which John Maynard Keynes called a "barbarous relic" long ago) and supply side economics, where the Laffer curve is used to justify the paradox that lower corporate taxes tend to increase government revenue. Based on these theories and the ten Operational Perversions cited above, the Wall Street Journal has made predictions, made judgments, and endorsed kindred spirits in its editorials that were truly remarkable. Examples include:

(1) In 1999: That the Dow Jones average would soon zoom up to 36,000 – see the 1999 book *Dow 36000: The New Strategy for Profiting from the Coming Rise in the Stock Market*, by Glassman and Hassett.

Burton G. Malkiel gushed in the WSJ, "*Dow 36,000* is a provocative and well-written treatise that cannot be dismissed. . . ." Soon thereafter, the Internet bubble burst and the Dow fell from a high of about 11,700 in January of 2000 to about 7,500 in September of 2002.

(2) From 2001 to 2010: That Bush's tax cuts of 2001 and 2003 would bring prosperity to all. Gauged at $1.3 Trillion over 10 years, it has successfully enriched the rich further. The WSJ is campaigning for making all of these nifty cuts permanent (especially the ones for the super rich) and its opinion echoes what the Heritage Foundation promises in its fairy-tale analysis: "Extending these tax cuts would boost U.S. GDP, employment, incomes, and federal tax collections consistently over the next 10 years." Yeah, sure.

(3) That there was never a housing bubble, and if there was one, it was the greedy homeowners' fault.

(4) That Saddam Hussein was the brain behind Al Qaeda and possessed WMDs ready to be sent America's way.

Based on their successes with predictive analysis and political savvy, Paul Krugman has stated the following compact assessment of the WSJ editorials:

(a)   The WSJ editorial page is wrong about everything.
(b)   If you think the WSJ editorial page is right about something, see rule #1.

The Stock Market

The Stock Market is a hybrid between a global marketplace and a casino with local gambling branches, so called stock exchanges. It exists in all countries where public ownership in corporations can be traded for private gain. We tend to associate the Stock Market with the noisy outcries of buy and sell orders by specialists "on the floor" of the New York Stock Exchange NYSE, with enigmatic hand signals and the seemingly chaotic blinking of computer screens surrounding this surreal arena. We may liken it to the Grand Bazaar in Istanbul. As far as it goes, this comparison is true, regarding the noise and the slightly shady atmosphere. But the most trades are not made in open markets but on virtual exchanges, such as the NASDAQ, where computer programs, eerily quiet, effect the trades. In addition, big blocks of stocks are periodically siphoned away from the active exchanges and, per invisible computer networks, steered into the largest investment banks, like the Goldman Sachs Group, which then pair buyers and sellers within their own system, usually in big chunks and away from the public spotlight, so that winners and losers remain anonymous.

As a market place, the Stock Market (more precisely, any of its actual and virtual trading exchanges) is governed by the law of supply and demand, which takes a special form here, the jostling of "asks and bids." A seller floats his shares in a company at a certain price, the "ask," while buyers offer to purchase them at a (lower) "bid." When the seller budges a little and/or the buyers move their bid up, the happy event of ask = bid may occur and a trade takes place. In this way, a stock market is not different from a bazaar, where the shop owner and his customer haggle and posture and scoff at each other, until they shake and the carpet changes owners. The price of the carpet is the sum of the cost of making it, or of buying it whole-sale, plus storage and transportation and booth fees, taxes, etc., plus some more or less arbitrary surcharge, determined by what the seller thinks he can get away with. For stocks, however, the market value is not simply calculated as if it were a manufactured asset like a carpet with a (more or less) objective value. That's where the analogy to the casino comes into play.

To understand this fully, let's see what factors decide the bid and ask price of a stock, and how you, too, can make money, not by working hard, but by investing wisely. Some diligent analysts prefer the "fundamental analysis," where income and outlays, products, management, sales channels and other company fundamentals are being assessed and used to compute a share price. Others prefer the "technical analysis" of charting price trends and using statistical indicators to make their buy or sell recommendations. However, says a third group of experts, either way it doesn't matter, because in the long run the stock market behaves "efficiently" and has figured in both the fundamentals and the statistical trends before you can make serious money. Therefore, by far the most important method for individual investors like you and me is the "emotional analysis," also known as the "I have my own system" syndrome. Based on what we read in newspapers ("panic or euphoria?"), which people we like to listen to (Nobelist Paul Krugman or Mad Money host Jim Cramer), what stuff we find attractive ("Apple's products are really cool"), and whom we want to succeed ("I only buy stocks of green companies"), we make our buying decisions. In short, we take our loves, hates, prejudices, and other pieces of emotional intelligence and guess what will happen in the Stock Market. Just like a gambler playing roulette will apply a rule such as this one: "It has now been Red five times, so naturally I'll bet on Black!"

If you are a risk taker or simply want to win a lot of money in a hurry, you should dare the market and predict the short term movements of your favorite stocks. Bet on them from hour to hour, thus becoming a day trader. Or buy options, which are like betting tickets for horse races: you don't ride the horse, instead you buy the possibility of making money if "your" horse wins. Or buy into a hedge fund, which must be a good deal, because its managers are rich! Or short a stock about which you fervently hope it'll go down soon, because you just hate that company (ever since you were laid off by them).

Because you probably own an IRA or a 401(k) account, or are vested in other market-dependent retirement schemes, the charging Bulls and slumping Bears of the Stock Market will be with you as long as you live and may well determine the cost and quality of your casket.

The Cubicle

Most corporate citizens work in cubicles. The name comes from its cubic shape, although a modern cubicle may be rectangular and have walls of different heights, built on different floor plans and with different furniture. As a piece of real estate, most important for the quality of a cubicle are location, size, and equipment. For instance, prime cubicle real estate is at the corner of a cubicle farm with the entrance facing a window, rather than another cubicle on a busy walkway. If you are a supervisor or department manager, you may not yet qualify for an office (one with an actual door), but your cubicle may have more floor space and be furnished with a small table and two hard plastic chairs for guests, in addition to your own ergonomic chair.

Cubicles have been compared to prison cells, and cubicle dwellers to convicts and inmates. Just as prisoners begin, after a while, to decorate their cells with personal items such as baby pictures, teddy-bears, artificial flowers, and a bible, so will inmates of corporate cubicles add their own sentimental touches around the 200 to 250 cubic feet they call their own during the workday. For a man, a small picture of his wife is most common, next to calendar glossies of cars, motorcycles, and boats. Women prefer pictures of their children, their mother, and a print of a dream house under an unrealistically blue sky.

A cubicle is not a dream house. Nevertheless, it does provide some limited privacy. It is limited by the height of the surrounding wall, which in technical jobs is about 5 feet, for sales, marketing, and services reps about 3 feet. Limited as well is the use of the computer: for company purposes only - please no private emails! At the same time, a cubicle inhabitant is able to hear what is going on in the neighborhood and, like a desert dog, he will periodically stand up on his hind legs and curiously peek around over the cubicle wall, a human periscope, without being much noticed himself. Juicy details about the commotion he has heard in this submarine mode will be revealed during his next trip to the Water Cooler.

In conversations at the Water Cooler employees complain about their cubicle – size, location, equipment, and most about: being boxed in. The art of cubicle life, the secret of using it for one's advantage, is this: live and work within it while *thinking outside the box*. This phrase does not mean that you'll make your cubicle life more tolerable by imagining a better life outside of it, for instance by thinking about riding through a countryside on a fancy motorcycle, or by fantasizing about that dream house under an unrealistically blue sky. Instead, *thinking outside the box* is the art of imagining new ways and means for the company to be successful, of having thoughts that have eluded others and that, therefore, are not yet part of the tool box of acknowledged company routines. Of course, *thinking outside the box* will have to be followed by *doing outside the box* and, most importantly, by succeeding better than routine box-thinking that has until now been done by your colleagues boxed up in their cubicles. Thus, for all the leveling equality the cubicle provides, it is at the same time, *ex negativo*, the reason that the most ambitious inmates attempt to leave its confines, at least by thinking outside of it, and so, as a reward, be able to leave it physically as well and gain a real office, one with a door and more privacy. In such offices, *thinking outside the box* is much more rare and often deemed no longer necessary.

But, it bears repeating: Almost every corporate citizens spends his time at work sitting in a cubicle, his very own box, where he is facing another box, his computer. After work, he will enter a third box, his car or the compartment of a train, and ride home, which is yet another box where he enjoys a limited privacy. In the end of his life there awaits another box, the final one, for which the cubicle has, during his long work life in a corporation, prepared him well.

The Water Cooler

The Water Cooler is the one member of the Corporation that everybody knows and meets regularly, often several times a day. Centrally located, close to the restrooms and next to the coffee station, the Water Cooler's most frequent visitors are the Corporate Gentleman, the Loquacious, the Wannabe, the Know-It-All, and the Busybody. Always present are Gossip and the Corporate Spirit.

Even to an observer without knowledge in group psychology, it is clear that the Water Cooler plays a role similar to the pub at the corner of 3rd and Main Street, where tall tales are told to strangers and sorrows drowned in drinks. It is the place where everybody knows everybody. That pub at 3rd and Main has replaced the well in the middle of a village, where the elders sipped their coffee and reminisced about the old times, and the young ones bragged about their plans for the future. In congregations such as these, the pursuit of truth and beauty is not the topic. Instead, rumors and mischievousness beget gossip, especially about those not present – where are they anyway? Do they think they are better than us? Above it all, over the pub and the well and the Water Cooler there hovers a feeling of community and belonging. This sense of togetherness may be a tribal bond or a religious belief, or simply friendship. But in a company the hovering is clearly performed by the Corporate Spirit himself.

Scholars have likened the Water Cooler to the Golden Calf in Genesis 32. When Moses returned from his meeting with his angry God on Mount Sinai, he severely criticized his people for congregating about the Golden Calf, dancing, drinking, and having a gay old time. According to Scripture, up to 3000 team members were executed as punishment. To top it off, God sent the plague.

Some less drastic occurrences have been reported about gatherings around the Water Cooler. In one instance, a functional manager X, who had just had a tense meeting with his general manager Y, returned to his office, and on his way to getting some coffee passed the Water Cooler. There the Know-It-All had already reported (how he knew nobody knew) that X had just been dressed down by general manager Y because of unmet sales quota. Upon which the Corporate Gentleman had advised caution and quiet, but then talked about the day when he had had an important audience with, no, not the general manager, but the vice president of sales himself, and they had strategized about this and that. The Wannabe chimed in with an unrelated story, which the Loquacious repeated in colorful words as if what the Wannabe had said was the plot from a comedy. And wasn't life in a corporation nothing if not a comedy? The Loquacious couldn't stop repeating this witticism. The Busybody interrupted, "No, it's a tragedy," and everybody laughed and the spirit was high because it was dress-down Friday afternoon.

The punishment following this idle chat was a different kind of dressing down. It was meted out by the functional manager X, mentioned above, a typical representative of middle management, a man even less secure in his position than Moses was in his role between an irritated god and those merrily dancing around the golden calf. The five aforementioned characters, the nosy Know-It-All, the smooth Corporate Gentleman, the ambitious Wannabe, the wordy Loquacious, and the Busybody, were called into a conference room. There, functional manager X began his reprimands not with swords (like Moses' Levites had done after the golden-calf disaster), but with words that are the most feared in a corporate setting when coming from your manager: "I am disappointed in you."

Note about the author:

After leaving the comfortable groves of academe, Wulf Rehder worked in several US corporations, from Fortune 500 company to start-up, first in research and development and finally as a vice president. His experiences have ranged from fascinating and exciting to disheartening. Disheartening was the irony-free seriousness of corporate life, exciting some of the research, fascinating the encounters with corporate characters. Of these, the most memorable ones are captured in this book.

Other books by Wulf Rehder:

Der deutsche Professor – Handbuch für Studierende, Lehrer, Professoren, und solche, die es werden wollen (3rd edition, 2017)

Hallo Herr Goethe – Phantastische Emails seit Adam und Eva (2015)

Neue Märchen der Geschwister Grimm – Für große und kleine Leute (2016)

Quisquilien zu Thomas Mann – Glossen und Gedankenkrümel (2017)

For comments and corrections, please make contact via email at wulfrehder@gmail.com